PEARLS OF WISDOM

Some Sayings of the Great Sufis
and
Their Short Biographies

by

Alhaj Prof. Dr. Khwaja Anwar Ullah Khan

KITAB BHAVAN
New Delhi - 2 (India)

KITAB BHAVAN
Publishers, Exporters & Importers
1784, Kalan Mahal, Darya Ganj
New Delhi - 110 002 [India]

Phones : *3274686, 3263383*
Telex : *31-63106 ALI IN*
Fax : *91-11-3263383*

ISBN 81-7151-201-1

First Edition 1995

Laser Typesetting at:
Laser Track
1784, Kalan Mahal, Darya Ganj
New Delhi-110 002 [India]

Published by:
Nusrat Ali Nasri for Kitab Bhavan
1784, Kalan Mahal, Darya Ganj
New Delhi - 110 002 [India]

Printed in India at:
Seema Offset Press
Chooriwalan
Delhi - 6 [India]

"Mercy descends at the mention of the pious"
-prophet *MOHAMMAD PBH.*

"Imam Yusuf Hamadani-advised some people,
who asked him what should they do when the
Saints have passed away from earth, "to read
eight pages **of the sayings every day.**"

CONTENTS

PREFACE   viii

(1) HAZRAT OWAIS QARNI
Visited Medina in 17H/638 A.D..Contemporary of
the Prophet PBH   1

(2) HAZRAT KH. HASAN BASRI
From 21H to 110H   2

(3) HAZRAT IMAM JAFER SADIQ
From 80 H/699 A.D. or 83H/702 A.D. to the old
age of 65 or 68 years   4

(4) HAZRAT RABIA BASRI
95H/714 A.D. to 185/801 A.D.   11

(5) HAZRAT MALIK IBN DINAR AL SANI
Died in 130H/748 A.D   12

(6) HAZRAT SUFYAN SURI
From 95H/714 A.D. or 96 or 97H to 161/788 A.D   13

(7) HAZRAT SHEIKH DAUD TAI
Died in 160H/777 A.D. or 163H/780 A.D   14

(8) HAZRAT SHEIKH MARUF KARKHI
Died in 200H/815 A.D   16

(9) HAZRAT HABIB AJAMI
From 156H to 272H.   17

(10) HAZRAT ZUNNUN OF EGYPT
From 180H/794 A.D. to 246H/861 A.D.   18

(11) HAZRAT SIRI AL SAQTI
Died in 253H/867 A.D. or 257H/870 A.D.   19

(12) HAZRAT BAYAZID BISTAMI
From 128H/746 A.D. to 261H/874 A.D.or 264H/
878 A.D.   20

(13) HAZRAT IBRAHIM BIN ADHAM
     From 179H/795 A.D. to 261H/874 A.D   22

(14) HAZRAT SUHAIL TASTARI
     rom 200H/815 A.D. or 203H/818 A.D. to 283H/896
     A.D   23

(15) HAZRAT JUNAID BAGHDADI
     Died in 298H/910 A.D   24

(16) HAZRAT MUMSHAD ULVA DINWARI
     Died in 299H   25

(17) HAZRAT HUSAIN BIN MANSUR HALLAJ
     From 244H/858 A.D. to 309H   26

(18) HAZRAT ABU BAKR SHIBLI
     Born in 247H/861 A.D   27

(19) HAZRAT ABU ALI AHMAD BIN MOHAMMAD
     Died in 321H/937 A.D   28

(20) HAZRAT USMAN SAEED
     Died in 373H/983 A.D   29

(21) HAZRAT ABUL HASAN KHIRQANI
     Born in 914 A.D   30

(22) HAZRAT ABU SAEED BIN KHAIRI
     Died in 440H/1047 A.D   31

(23) HAZRAT DATA GANJ BAKSH
     From 400H to 465H   32

(24) HAZRAT IMAM GHIZALI
     From 445H/1059 A.D. to 505H/1111 A.D   37

(25) HAZRAT ABDUL QADIR JEELANI
     From 470H/1077 A.D. to 561H/1166 A.D   38

(26) HAZRAT FARID UDDIN ATTAR
     From 1140 A.D. to 1226 A.D   40

(27) HAZRAT SHEIKH MOIN UDDIN CHISTI
     From 536H/1141 A.D. to 633H/1236 A.D   41

(28) HAZRAT LAL SHAHBAZ QALANDER
From 538H/1144 A.D. to 633H/1236 A.D   44

(29) HAZRAT BAKHTIAR KAKI
From 583H/1187 A.D. to 633H/1235 A.D   46

(30) HAZRAT BABA FARID GANJ SHAKAR
From 569H/1173 A.D. or 584H/1180 A.D.
to 664H   48

(31) HAZRAT SHEIKH BAHA UDDIN ZAKARIA
From 578H/1182 A.D. to 661H/1262 A.D   53

(32) HAZRAT SABIR KALYARI
Born in 592H   55

(33) HAZRAT MAULANA JALAL UDDIN RUMI
From 1207 A.D. to 1273 A.D   56

(34) HAZRAT BU ALI QALANDER
From 605H/1208 A.D. to 724H/1324 A.D Contemporary of Hazrat Kh. Nizam Uddin Aulia   113

(35) HAZRAT KH. NIZAM UDDIN AULIA
From 636H to 725H   116

(36) HAZRAT BURHAN UDDIN GHARIB
From 636H to 725H   123

(37) HAZRAT MAKHDOOM JEHANIAN JEHAN GASHT
From 654H/1256 A.D. to 738H/1331 A.D   124

(38) HAZRAT SH. NASIR UDDIN CHIRAG DELHI
Died in 1367 A.D/768H   126

(39) HAZRAT KHWAJA OBED ULLAH AHRAR
From 805H to 895H   127

(40) HAZRAT NUR UDDIN ABDUL-REHMAN JAMI
From 817H/1414 A.D. to 898H/1494 A.D   130

(41) HAZRAT MOHAMMAD SAEED SARMAD
Born in 1618 A.D. Contemporary of Emporer
Alamgir   131

BIBLIOGRAPHY   132

PREFACE

This book **PEARLS OF WISDOM** depicts the Sufi thoughts. The great Sufis from the early period of Islam, till the beginning of this century, have influenced the thinking of the common man, inculcating in them piety, religious tolerance, patience, charity, simplicity, humbleness and many other good qualities which make this world worth living. To create intarest of the readers, a short life-history of the great Sufis is incorporated. In making the present selection of names of the Sufis, in this book, I have indulged in the generosity of my critics. No doubt, there were other great Sufis whose names are not included in this book and their sayings as well. After all, this is the first edition & an humble attempt on my part. Insha Alla, names of other great Sufis will be included in subsequent edition, according to the valuable suggestions of readers of this book. Their period and the country to which they belonged is noted, although their teachings have been universal. According to the dates of birth and death, where available, their names are noted in this book, more-or-less in a chronological order.

Three main characters of Sufis exist in the Persian word "FIQR". F stands for "Faqa", means "Fasting", I is silent in the word, Q stands for "Qinayat", which means "Patience" and R stands for "Riyaz" which depicts prolonged hours of worship (of God), more than what is required in following "Shariat". The Prophet Mohammad PBH had mystical awareness. He had mystical experience of a Super-Natural Presence. As such Sufism can be traced back to the time of the Prophet PBH. It is said that Prophet Mohammad PBH invested Hazrat Ali with a cloak (Kharqa) and initiated him in the esoteric mysteries, imparting him spiritual wisdom, which is beyond all formal worldly learning. Hazrat Ali too is considered as the first great Sufi. They followed the principles of "FIQR".

The Sufis were mainly guided by the Holy Quran, Hadith and the practices of Sahaba (contemporaries of the Prophet PBH) Tabaeen (contemporaries of Sahaba), Taba-Tabaeen (contemporaries of Tabaeen). Sufism is thus a developed culture based on deep religious knowledge (Ilm) and practice (Amal). But according to Hazrat Kh. Moin Uddin Chisti, Sufism, is neither knowledge alone, or form alone. It is the Ethical Discipline of Mystics. Knowledge (Ilm) is acquired through the physical efforts of eyes and ears, or through intuition (divine) - "Ilham". The Prophets acquired knowledge directly from behind the veil (hidden God) through angel or through manifestation of God in shape or form, as in the case of Moses. This in fact is Gnosis-Maarfat, of the Reality (Haqiqat).

In their teachings to the followers, the Sufis referred many a times to the Holy Quran and Hadith. By and large Sufis did follow strictly Shariat, which means formal laws of Islam. The other method of worship is called Tariqat, which means Path, the Ethical Discipline and which emphasized meditation and Sama-audition of religious music. Sama is part of the method of worship of the Chistia sect, though not practiced in the Qadaria section, an equally important section of Sufism. The Chistia sect was introduced in the Indian subcontinent by Hazrat Moin Uddin Chisti, who finally migrated to Ajmere. Chisht is a village near Hirat (Khurasan, in medieval period). Sama has an Exoteric aspect and an Esoteric aspect. The exoteric aspect applies to common people and novices. It is mainly dependent on the musical instruments and poetry. In case of the Sufis of Chistia Sect, it is the Esoteric aspect of Sama, which plays a significant role in worship. It becomes a source of Ecstasy (Wajd), in which they may dance in a typical Sufi way or may even tear their garments. They loose self control, in the latter condition. There are other important sects like Naqshbandia and Suhrwardia with their own originalities in their practices.

It will not be out of place to mention that the word Sufi has originated from the word Sufva, which means wool, as the Sufis generally dressed themselves in woolen overalls. Others think that the origin is from "Ahl Safva", that pious group of persons who used to sit on a low platform in Masjid Nabavi from the time of Prophet (PBH). This was a group of humble, pious, patient and poor persons. Such persons still occupy, generally during prayer time a platform behind the grave of the Prophet (PBH) and his companions Hazrat Abu Bakr Siddiq, (RAA) and Hazrat Umar (RAA) - the first two Khalifas.

The Sufis have grades, like Salik, Qutub, Majzub, Wali and others and perform assigned spiritual duties accordingly. Sufism influenced Arabia, Iraq, Iran, Asia Minor and the Indian sub-continent and wherever Islam spread out. Persia made outstanding contributions to Sufism. The political renaissance of Persia under the 10th Century dynasties of Suffarids & Samanids brought the revival of the Persian language. The earliest Persian book on Sufism is said to be "Kashful-Mahjub", written by Hazrat Ali Abul Hasaan Hajweri-Data Sahab, who ultimately settled in Lahore, at the instruction of his "Pir".

The concept of Sufism is based on two theories: (1) Hama Ost i.e. God exists in every thing and, (2) Az

Hama Ost i.e. every thing is from God. The other division of Sufis is based on the concept of (a) WAHDATUL-WUJUD, which means UNITY OF BE-INGS, and (b) WAHDATUL SHAHUD, which means Unity of Witnesses.

The object of this book is to give an opportunity of spiritual benefit and spiritual purification to those who are inclined to follow the simplicity of Sufi's lives, their advice and teachings. It is not limited to persons of a particular faith, but persons of all faiths can be benefited by them. True spiritualism is as rare these days as Philosopher-stone. Yet the Prophet Mohammad PBH said that "Mercy descends at the mention of the Pious". Some people appeared before Imam Yusuf Hamadani, and requested him to let them know, as to what should be done when Saints have left this world and passed away. He advised them to read eight pages of their sayings every day. As a matter of fact, in India, Islam spread by the teachings of these great Sufis of the subcontinent and not by influence of sword, or patronizing or pressurizing by the ruling Muslim kings, some of whom did not follow the teachings of Islam strictly.

Though this book was started with the main idea to emphasize the teachings of Maulana Rum, as depicted in his verses of the Mathnavi, containing over two thousand verses. The Mathnavi is so concise and full of Islamic teachings that it has been referred by some, as the Holy Quran in Persian language, though it is not a translation of the Holy Quran at all.

But the teachings of Sufi Shah Bu Ali Qualander of Panipat are also included in some details. He was contemporary of Hazrat Nizamuddim Aulia. The sayings of earlier Sufis of Arabia, Iraq and Iran are noted in brief.

I wish and pray that the book , Pearls of Wisdom may benefit and guide us all in our worldly and spiritual life. Amen.

For the sake of brevity, certain abbreviations have been used in the text, such as "H" stands for HAZRAT, M. for Maulana, H against numbers stands for Hijri, H against a saying stands for Hadith and Q against a saying stands for the Holy Quran, Sh. stands for SHEIKH PBH for Peace be on Him, RAA for Razi Allaho Anho which means God approved him.

My thanks are due to Ms. Linda Gless who worked hard in typing and recording this book on a computer. I am thankful to all those persons who took interest in reading proofs of this book. I cannot fail to mention in this conection the names of Mr. Yamin Uddin Haqqi of Lahore and Ms. Kaneez Fatma Khan of Kanpur. Both of them took great interest in reading the manuscript and giving their valuable suggestions.

HAZRAT OWES QARNI

HAZRAT OWES QARNI BIN AAMIR was a noble man of Yemen. He adopted Islam in absentia, as he could not come to meet the Prophet, on account of feeble health of his old mother whom he was serving. He came to Medina in 17 H 838 A.D. He came from Yemen and brought a battalion of army with him to meet and help Hazrat Umar Faruq. Then he left for Basra and met Hazrat Umar Faruq again. He took part in the battle of Azerbaijan. On return he fell ill and died suddenly. Some say that he took part in the battle of Safeen, along with Hazrat Ali. He had 40 wounds and died in Damascus. Other say he died in Holy Mecca. He was a very pious man, and Prophet Mohammed praised him in his absence.

He said:

(1)   Hold fast the book of God (Holy Quran).

(2)   The souls of Momins recognize each other, though the persons may not have been introduced or met earlier.

(3)   Be in the company of good people of Ummat.

(4)   Recite repeatedly "The Darud" on the Prophet.

(5)   Do not be unmindful of death.

(6)   Do not abandon fellowship, otherwise you will be cast out of religion.

(7)   My friend is my Seclusion.

(8)   We can know the inner condition of man correctly from his exterior.

HAZRAT HASAN BASRI

HAZRAT HASAN BASRI was born in 21 H and lived until 110H He was, as such among Tabaeen . He was a venerable man, associated with performance of Miracles. His Father's name was Musa Raee. He was born in the time of Khalifa Umar Faruq in Medina. His father was a released slave of Ansari & mother was a slave girl.

When he was brought before Hazrat Umar Faruq, being a handsome infant, he suggested that his name should be Hasan. Hazrat Hasan dealt in the sale of jewelry and earned a lot through this business. But he was over-powered by the love of God, He distributed all his assets in charity and got busy in worship of God, leaving all the worldly affairs. He was very particular about Sunnat-e-Nabavi. Being afraid of God, he used to cry very often. He died at the age of 89 in Basra, during the reign of Hashim Bin Abdul Malik.

Hazrat Hasan Basri said:

(1) The end ofthe world and beginning of the life to come, is in the tomb.

(2) Evil company degenerates the seeker.

(3) Accumulation of wealth is worse than drinking wine, which is prohibited in scriptures.

(4) Be not close to a king, however patronizing he may be. His behavior towards you can change at any time.

(5) Do not sit alone with a woman (Na-Mahram), however pious she may be like Hazrat Rabia

Basri and you may be giving lessons to her.

(6)   Do not dislike worldly things & consider them lowly & useless.

(7)   Keep your ego under control.

(8)   Be cautious of the instruments of music (music itself) because man cannot keep his heart under control on hearing music and he falters.

(9)   The real patience and piety are those which are for the sole approval of God-the-Great. As such there is no aspect of profit or loss for self.

(10) A dog has ten superb qualities (which can be compared with the good qualities of pious men):

I.   He has no house of his own - like men of patience.

II.   He can remain hungry.

III. He remains alert at night, like pious people (who worship at night).

IV.   He has no personal property - like pious people.

V.   He is always faithful to his master, like faithful persons.

VI.   He sits on lowly places without hesitation, like humble persons.

VII. He goes to another place when his sleeping place has been usurped. It is like contented people.

VIII. He comes forward waging his tail, if a piece of bread is thrown before him, not with standing he might have been scolded earlier.

It is the quality of good natured people.

IX. He sits aloof from the master (unless spoiled) when the latter is taking his meals. It is the quality of holy and contented persons.

X. When he leaves his residence once for the good, he does not return to it, like strong minded persons.

HAZRAT IMAM JAFER SADIQ

HAZRAT IMAM JAFER SADIQ - The sixth Imam of Shias. His ancestry goes from father's side up to Hazrat Ali and from mother's side to Hazrat Abu Bakr Siddiq. His date of birth is controversial - 80 or 83 H. He was born in Medina. For 14 years he was educated by his grandfather Imam Zainul Abidin and for 34 years by father, Imam Mohammed Baqer and for 27 years by his maternal grandfather Hazrat Qasim, simultaneously. He followed a holy life and kept himself away from politics. He was contemporary of Khalifa Mansur Abbas. He was called by him once to his Durbar and given special honor. Imam Jafer asked him not to be called again, as it disturbed his prayers to God. He spent greater part of his life in Medina. He died at the age of 65 or 68 in Medina and was buried in Jannat-ul-Baqi.

Hazrat Imam Jafer Sadiq said:

* God is not met till we are extremely distressed for Him and seek Him just as a drowning man.

* It is a sin to be vain about your worship.

* He advised to remain aloof from 5 types of persons. (1)   A liar, as you will always remain haughty with him; (2)A fool, as you will always be at a loss, however, the fool may want to benefit you; (3) A miser, as he will waste your precious time; (4) A coward as he will get aside in the time of need; and (5) A hypocrite, as he will sell your teachings for a nominal gain.

SAYINGS FROM "THE LANTERN OF THE PATH" by H. JAFER AL-SADIQ. Published by "Elementary Book Ltd". Longmead, Shaftesbury, Dorset. U.K.

* LOWERING GAZE- There is nothing more gainful than lowering one's gaze, from things which God has forbidden, unless witnessing of Majesty and Glory of God which has already come to heart.

* KNOWLEDGE- It is the basis of every sublime state and culmination of every high station.

* JUDGEMENT- Giving judgement is not permissible to one who has not been endowed by God with quality of inner Purity and Sincerity in both hidden and visible actions.

* CAUTION- Whoever is denied caution, is not a man of Knowledge even if he can split hairs in dealing with obscure items of knowledge.

* THANKFULNESS   - The lowest level of the gratitude is to see that the blessing comes from God, irrespective of the cause for it, without the heart being attached to that cause.

* RECITING QURAN- The person who really recited the Quran needs 3 things: (1) a fearful heart, (2) a tranquil and receptive body, (3) an appropriate

place to recite.

* DRESS- The best adornment of the Believer's garment is Precaution, the most blessed garment is Belief.

* TRUTHFULNESS   - It is a light which radiates its reality in its own world. It is like sun, from whose reality every thing seeks light without any reduction in this reality.

* SINCERITY- Lies in all distinguished actions. It is a notion that starts with acceptance, and ends with God's pleasure

* PRECAUTION(Taqwa)- Has 3 factors: (1) Precaution observed by dependence on God, (2) Precaution of doubtful matter and forbidden things, (3) Precaution of the Fire and Punishment, which results on not leaving forbidden things.

* GOD FEARINGNESS - Close the gates of your limbs and senses to all which will harm your Heart, and bring in its wake grief and regret on the day of Judgement.

* SOCIAL INTERACTION-. Courteous and Social relations with God's Creation while avoiding all acts of disobedience to Him, is a sign of God's generosity to His bondsmen.

* SLEEP- Sleep the sleep of the mindful. Do not sleep the sleep of the headless. For the mindful among the astutes sleeps only for rest and does not purposely sleep through laziness.

* INTENTION - The person who has a sincere intention is the the one who has a sound heart. A sound heart is free from thoughts about

forbidden things.

* CLARIFICATION OF TRUTH AND FALSEHOOD- This Precaution is desirable for all parties. In it is gathered all goodness and maturity.

* RECOGNITION- Do not forsake certainty for doubt and what is clear for what is hidden. Do not pass judgement on what you cannot see, only because of something you are told about it.

* DUTIFULNESS TO PARENTS- It comes to the bondsman with correct knowledge of God. It brings more quickly the pleasure of God.

* HUMILITY- It embraces every precious, noble rank and high position.

* EATING- There is nothing more harmful to the believer's heart than having too much food, for it causes arousal of (evil) desires.

* PRIDE- Whoever is proud of himself and his actions has strayed off the path of right guidance and has claimed what does not belong to him.

* PROSTATION IN PRAYER- A person who performs prostration (sajda), does not lose God at all, even if it is done only once in his entire life.

* HUMBLENESS TOWARDS GOD- Be a slave to God in your innermost being, fearful and humble to Him in action, as you are. His bondsman by word and claim.

* AL-SALAM(Peace)- is one of the names of God, who has entrusted it to His creation, so that they would make use of it in their behavior, trust and contract for the soundness of social relations.

* REPENTENCE- is the rope of God and mainstay of His concern for His servant, who must show repentence in every state.

* SILENCE- Lock your tongue to the speech which is not absolutely necessary especially when you do not find any one worth talking to, except when you are specifically talking about matters, with reference to God.

* INTELLECT - The man of intellect submits to what is true and just in his speech. He refrain from what is false and opposes it in his speech

* ENVY- Envious man harms himself, before he harms the person he envies. (As was the case with Iblis).

* GREED- The soundest thing is scrupulousness and the most corrupt is greed.

* CORRUPTION- Of the outward comes from corruption of the Inward.

* WELL-BEING- Seek well being (Salamati) from God, wherever you are, in whatever state you may be, for your faith, your heart and ultimate outcome of your affairs.

* WORSHIP- Persevere in performing the customs and obligations in worship.

* REST- The believer aquires true rest, only when he meets God (Ibadat) although true rest may also be obtained by Silence and retreat.

* HUNGER- Which melts fleshy appetite, temptation, and brings wakefulness which illuminates the heart, and cleanses the spirit.

* AVARICE- Do not covet anything avariciously, for

if you ignore it, it will come to you anyway, if it is destined to be yours.

* GNOSTIC- The intimate conversation of the gnostic posseses 3 roots - Fear, Hope and Love. Love is the branch of Gnosis (Maarfat).

* FASTING- The Prophet said fasting is a protection from calamities of this world and a veil from punishment of the next.

* ABSTINENCE- consists of leaving every thing which could distract you from God. It is the key to the door of the next world and freedom from Fire.

* RELUCTANCE TO ACT- A person who feels reluctant to act falls short of what is correct.

* TAKING AND GIVING- It behoves the believer when he takes something, he should take rightfully. If he gives it should be for a right purpose, in a right way and from his rightful possession.

* BROTHERHOOD- Three things are rare in every age: (1) Brotherhood in God's faith, (2) a devout affectionate wife, who helps you in God's faith, (3) a rightly guided son.

* CONSULTATION- If you find 5 things - intellect, knowledge, experience, good counsel and precaution in a person, then make use of them and be resolute and rely on God.

* PARDON- To Pardon some one when you have the power to punish, was one of the customary practice of Messengers and is the secret of the God-fearing.

* EXHORTATION- The best form of exhortation is
  when words used do not go beyond the limits of
  truth and actions performed do not go beyond the
  limits of sincerity.

* ADVISE (wasiyat) - The best advice and the most
  necessary is that you do not forget your Lord and
  you remember Him whether sitting or standing.

* DISCIPLINE - He who suhdues his passions
  wants God's pleasure.

* CONTEMPLATION OF DEATH- It kills the desires,
  cuts off the roots of heedlessness, strengthens the
  heart with God's promise of life (hereafter).

* ENTRUSTING ONESELF TO GOD- One who
  entrusts his affairs to God is in eternal rest, and
  a constant carefree life.

* FEAR AND HOPE- Fear is the custodian of heart
  and Hope is the intercession of the self, whoever
  knows God fears Him and sets his Hope in Him.

* CONTENTMENT- is when a person is contented
  with what he loves and what he hates. It is a ray
  of light of Gnosis. He who is contented has
  annihilated all his desires.

* PATIENCE- It reveals whatever light and purity
  there is in the innermost being of God's servant.
  While anxiety shows darkness and bereftness
  inside them.

* GNOSIS(Marfat)- The gnostic (Arif) is with the
  people while his heart is with God.

* LOVE OF GOD- when it takes possession of the
  innermost being of God's bondsman. it empties
  him of every pre-occupation except rememberance
  of God.

HAZRAT RABIA BASRI

HAZRAT RABIA BASRI- From 95 H / 714 A.D. to 185 H / 801 A. D. She is counted among Aulia. She was born in a poor family. Somebody, in her childhood, kidnapped her and sold her. On account of her pious nature she was set free. She at first prayed in the forest. When she returned to Basra, those who believed in her, spirtuality surrounded her, to get blessings from her and spiritual education. Some of them were the famous Sufi Malik bin Dinar, Mohaddis Sufyan Sur & Sufi Balkhi. She was a great pious lady and many miracles are attributed to her. She used to pray every night on the roof of her house, not for getting heaven in after life, but to see the underlying beauty of God. When the last moment of life came up it is said that she asked everybody to leave her and let the Messenger of God come in. As soon as they left her she was heard uttering "Kalma-e-Shahadat".

Hazrat Rabia Basri said:

(1)   It is only when the Lord confers His power on the sinner that he is urged to confess and is penitent. Therefore the Lord accepts his repentance for his past sins.

(2)   Pain is the privilege of great devotees, who cherish it with joy.

(3)   The gift of the world and our anguish for God cannot lodge simultaneously in one and the same heart.

(4)   It does not behove a friend to will contrary to

the Will of the friend.

(5)   One talks of that thing very much, to which one is most attached.

(6)   For Spiritual attainment, leave everything, worldly, and only think of lasting love of God.

HAZRAT IBN DINAR AL SANI

He was son of a Persian slave from Sejestan (Kabul). He became a disciple of Hazrat Hasan Basri. He is mentioned as a reliable traditionalist by such early authorities as Anas Ibn Malik and Ibn Suri. He was noted as an early calligrapher of the Holy Koran. He died in 130 C/748 A.D.

Hazrat Malik Ibn Dinar came to be so named "Dinar" as it is stated that he stretched his hand down in the sea water and took out two Dinars from the mouth of a fish and passed them on to the marines who demanded fare from him, otherwise they would throw him overboard from the sailing ship. They hit him so much that first he became unconscious. When he became conscious they wanted to throw him for not paying the fare. It is said that many fish in the water at that moment swam close up to the ship, each with a gold Dinar in its mouth.

Saying of Hazrat Malik Bin Dinar:

"God loves most in any action, its ethics."

HAZRAT SUFYAN SURI

HAZRAT SUFYAN SURI- He was a learned man, a Sufi & Mohaddis of second century Hijri. His full name was Abu Abdulla Sufyan bin Saeed bin Maesraq AlSuri Alfufi.. He was born on Hijri 95 or 96 or 97. His initial education was from his father, who was a great learned man of his time. H. Sufyan refused government service and as such the Rulers were annoyed with him. He, Imam Hambal and Imam Abu Hanifa always had confrontations with the civil Rulers. As such H.Sufyan left Baghdad and went to Yemen. From there he went to Holy Mecca, where Amir of Mecca Mohammed bin Ibrahim protected him, somehow or other from the cruelty of the Khalifa of Baghdad. Even then, he had to leave for Basra and patch up with the Khalifa, by correspondence. He prepared himself to leave for Baghdad, but fell ill and died in 161 H. /778 A.D. at the age of 64. Some people thought that he was Shia earlier. H.Farid Uddin Attar has written a chapter about him in his book - Tazkiratul Aulia. He was contemporary of Imam Abu Hanifa. .He thought that the first Khalifa scored over Hazrat Ali.

Hazrat Sufyan Suri said:

(1) My sins are very insignificant, like a blade of grass, as compared to His mercy and benevolence.

(2) Worse than the sin against God, is the sin against man.

(3)   Refuse gifts from Rulers as it may lead to weakness in the sense of Justice.

(4)   Iman can increase & decrease as well.

(5)   In "Ablution" feet can be touched (Masah) over socks, instead of washing them.

(6)   Silent recital of Bismillah, carries greater weight than a loud uttering.

(7)   Jehad will last till the Day of Judgement.

HAZRAT SHEIKH DAUD TAI

HAZRAT SHEIKH DAUD TAI- His full name was Suleman Daud Bin Nasar Tai. He was a disciple of Imam-ul-Fiqa-Imam-e-Azam. He was Khalifa of Hazrat Habib Ajami. He was well versed both in worldly and spiritual education. He died in Baghdad and is buried over there.

Hazrat Habib al Rai converted him to Ascetic life. He was the one who threw his books in the river Euphrates and went into seclusion. It is said that he died between 160H/777 A.D. and 163 H/780 A.D.

He used to remain overwhelmed by inner grief and preferred seclusion than mixing with men.

Hazrat Abu Hanifa who was his teacher, once told him that "This is not the solution for you to hide in your house and keep absolute silence. The proper course for you is to sit at the feet of the Imams and listen to their propounding novel ideas. You should

attend what they have to say patiently, uttering not
a word". He remained in attendance before the
Imam for one year.

"This one year's patience, "is equivalent to 30
years of strenuous work" he remarked at the end of
that time. He was recipient of 20 Dinars in
inheritance. This he spent in 20 years. "I hold this
amount to secure the peace of mind". he explained.
"I can do with this until I die". His austerity was
to such an extent that he would dip bread in water
and when dissolved, he would sip water saying
"Between this and eating the bread, I can recite 50
verses of the Koran. Why should I waste my life". He
remained a bachelor through out saying that "since
he could not attend both his religious and worldly
duties, he would deceive his wife if he married. He
did not have time to comb his beard even. Khalifa
Harun Al Rasheed asked Hazrat Abu Yusuf to take
him to visit Hazrat Daud Tai. But he was refused
admission. He begged Hazrat Daud's mother to
intercede. Ultimately Khalifa Harun was granted an
audience on the intercession of Hazrat Daud's mother.
Khalifa Harun wept bitterly before Hazrat Daud.
Hazrat Daud did not accept any present in the form
of money. Hazrat Daud Tai died exactly after 20
years when the 20 Dinars were finished. He used to
spend one silver penny each day.

He used to say:

(1)   If you believe that God is with you, then do not
      be afraid of anybody. If you think that God is
      not with you, then do not covet an anybody's
      help.

(2)   Children are pleased with the cash (coins) and
      play with it.

(3) Run away from the worldly people, as they run
    away from the beasts.

(4) Get in the company of Religious people and see
    how little they spend on themselves and how
    they help others.

(5) Do not abandon your group (religious).

HAZRAT MARUF AL KARKHI

Hazrat Maruf Al Karkhi, Ibn Feroz Al Karkhi. He
was a great Sufi saint, in the time of Khalifa
MOTASSIN ABBASI. He was born of Christian
parents. There is a story of his conversion to Islam,
on his rejection of the Trinity principle, while still in
school. Later his parents too got converted to Islam.
His maternal grandfather was ruler of"Kokh" and
was a fire worshipper. He died in the year 200H/815
A.D. and was buried in Baghdad. His grave is still
honored and visited by people. He was a renowned
Sufi of Baghdad School of thought. He was a
humanitarian and full of humility. He could read
inner thoughts of others. After his death, men of all
religions claimed him as one of them, this included
men of Jewish, Christian and Muslim faith

HAZRAT HABIB AJAMI

HAZRAT HABIB AJAMI - Born in 156H / 272 A.D.. He was very rich in the beginning and earned his income from interest on loans to individuals. Two incidents turned him towards God, and he left taking interest, on loans. In one of these incidents, when he drowned himself in constant worship and prayers, he could not earn his daily bread. For ten days he returned home empty handed and made a plea before his wife that his employer will give wages after ten days. A miracle happened on the tenth day. When he returned home, thinking as to what excuse he would make then before his wife. Somebody during his absence at his house, delivered sumptuous food and 3 thousand Dinars, to his wife. As soon as his wife saw him on his return to the house, she told him, whose service are you doing that he has sent so much wages only for your 10 days service to him? Tears came to the eyes of Hazrat Ajmi, and he thought that God had given him so much, to his sinful servant for 10 days wages. His love and worship of God, with earnestness, increased to a great extent, after this miracle.

His famous sayings are:

(1)   One is required to have belief along with knowledge.

(2)   One who harbors no enmity towards others, in his heart, that heart will receive God's favor.

(3)   A true disciple (Sufi) is the one who is not attracted towards worldly affairs.

(4)   His motto was that "Envy and Love of the world

must disappear from the heart of a true seeker (of God)."

(5) God likes a person who has no malice in his heart towards anyone.

HAZRAT ZUNNUN OF EGYPT

HAZRAT ZUN NUN - His full name was Hazrat Abul Fazl Sobani bin Ibrahim. He was a Sufi saint of Egypt. He studied Medicine & Chemistry. His teacher was H.Sadun Misri. H.Zunnun traveled to Holy Mecca & Damascus. In his old age he was arrested and brought to Baghdad. In the end he was released at the order of Khalifa Al Mutawakkil. He returned to Egypt. He was called "Raes-al-Sufi", meaning leader of Sufis. He wrote a few books on Medicine & Chemistry. He wrote Poetry as well. H.Zunnun was a practical Sufi. He told about the stages of hurdles in elevating oneself spiritually. He gave details of living a life merging oneself in God (Fana Fillah)

HAZRAT ZUNNUN said:

(1) In the path of spirituality hope is born out of hopelessness.

(2) Solitude is the best teacher to the pursuer of the path of spiritualism.

(3) Do not hate one as a sinner, for there is no certainty that at the last breath, he may repent and God may accept his repentance.

(4) Repent not, for the past, nor worry for the future. Make most of the present, living in the remembrance of God.

(5) Without His Grace it is difficult to turn the heart to Him, and with His Grace it runs effortlessly on the Path.

(6) How can one, lost in Ecstasy, carry on worship.

(7) Ego was an obstruction in the spiritual progress. This can be controlled by prayers and suppression of ego.

(8) "Marfat" was another name of knowing the quality of Oneness of God.

(9) God bestows the quality of knowing the unknown, even the thoughts of others, to the friends of God (Aulia).

(10) The choicest person before God is one who has the greatest wisdom and wisdom lies in accepting the truth, however, it may come out of mouth of a person lower in worldly grade than himself.

HAZRAT SIRI AL SAQTI

HAZRAT SIRI AL SAQTI - His full name was Abul Hasan Bin Magas. He was maternal uncle of H Junaid Baghdadi, who was his disciple too and is buried in the Mausoleum of Alsaqti. He died at the age of 78 or 98 in the year 870 A.D. Imam Hanbli objected to his thought of the Holy Quran being of human origin. He was not very particular of religious teachings, in the matter of food or drinks.

Siri Saqti emphasized that there were two paths Tariqat and Shariyat.

HAZRAT BAYAZID BISTAMI

HAZRAT BAYAZID BISTAMI - Was born in 128H/ 746 A.D. He died in 261H./878 A.D. He was a great Sufi saint, in third century Hijri. His grandfather changed his religion of Star-worshiper to Islam. Hazrat Ba Yazid got spiritual teachings from H.Abu Ali Sindhi, who was not conversant with the Arabic language, Hazrat Bayazid taught him a few Ayats from the Holy Quran, and in return he got some spiritual secrets from Hazrat Abu Ali Al Sindhi. He was a Mohaddis. He did not write any book, but his 500 sayings have been preserved by his disciples. His grave is in Bastan. A big dome was constructed over it by Sultan Alkhani Mohammed in 1313 A. D.

HAZRAT BAYAZAD said:

(1) Lord dwells among the Broken hearts in the world. The dwelling place of the Lord is in the meek and humble hearts.

(2) Unless their renunciation is perfect, they shall not get entry in the path. (of Sufis)

(3) When He shall look at me, all the qualifications will be born in me

(4) Lord, be Bayazid's and deal with him as Thou will.

(5)   When God loves, He sends sufferings.

(6)   Better than a virtuous act is the company of the virtuous and worse than an evil act done is the company of the evil persons.

(7)   Depend solely not on your efforts, but on His Grace.

(8)   Consider the length of life as today only and no more.

(9)   Who is a saint? Who loves nothing besides God.

(10) One does not attain the spiritual elevation by leaving the practice of the Prophet, PBH, even though the non-performance of the Sunnat be due to ignorance.

(11) Who is humble:

   I.   One who eats food with his servants and the poor.

   II.   One who salutes the young.

   III.   One who milks goats and sheep himself.

   IV.   One who does not try to go ahead of the group, if walking in a group.

   V.   One who sits in the company of Faqirs.

   VI.   One who removes thorns and stones out of the Passage.

   VII. One who makes purchases of his needs in Bazaar himself.

(12) Lovers of God do not value Heaven. They are drowned in the love of God only

HAZRAT IBRAHIM BIN ADHAM

IBRAHIM BIN ADHAM - He was a great Sufi. He was initially a Prince of Ballakh. He adopted the life of a mendicant and was raised to a high level, spiritually. There is some controversy regarding the date of his birth and death. According to "Serai Aqtab" he was born in 281H / 894 A. D. Two incidents in his life changed its course. Once he saw or dreamed that a man was on the roof of his palace. When asked as to what he was doing at the roof, he told him that he was searching his camel. When Ibrahim told him that how did he expect a camel on the roof of a palace? He replied that "how do you expect to be a godly man when putting on royal rich clothes"? The second incident was that a person came up to his throne and sat nearby. When asked as to why he had come? He replied that he had come to stay in the inn. He was told that it was not an inn, but a palace. The man argued with Ibrahim bin Adham that "Your father, your grandfather, stayed here for some period and then went away. You too will go away and your son will stay here. Is it not then an inn?" After this incident Ibrahim got very perturbed, put on the dress of a mendicant and roamed about in the jungle. He stayed in a cave for 9 years in Neshapur. He roamed about in forest for a total period of 40 years.

Hazrat Ibrahim Bin Adham said:

(1)   Never feel proud of your praise.

(2)   Dishonestly earned food divests you of the spiritual experience.

(3)   Knowledre. if not embellished with faith is of
      no worth

(4)   What is the reason that our prayers are not
      accepted: (a) Not recognizing the LORD, as to
      follow and obey His commandments; (b) Not
      following the scriptures; (c) Non gratitude
      towards Him; (d) Not acting as to avoid Hell;
      (e) Not dealing with Satan as enemy; (f) No
      preparation for death; (g) No lessons from the
      graves of dead parents; (h) You know you have
      many faults, yet you try to find faults with
      others. How do you expect then, that God will
      grant your prayer.

(5)   Earn your bread by labor and do not depend on
      the charity of others.

For Many years he stayed in Holy Mecca; it is
stated that he took part in the battle of Rum and
died there. Others say that he died in Syria in 892
A.D.

HAZRAT SUHAIL TASTARI

HAZRAT SUHAIL TASTARI - Full name Abu
Mohammed Suhail Bin Abdulla bin Yusuf. He was
born in Tastar (Ahwaz). Ibne Khalqan disagrees with
date of birth. He said that H. Suhail was born in
200 H. / 815 A. D. Hazrat Suhail was the disciple
of H.A. Suri and H.Abu Umar bin Alula-learned
people. He was very particular about Piety and
Discipline. Some learned men (Alim) of Ahwaz were
very1critical of his Magazine - Risalai-Aqaid, which
concerned with the Duty-bound Repentance. On this

account he had to pass the period of rest of his life, away from his home. Hazrat Suhail did not write any book himself, but his disciple Mohammed Bin Salim has compiled one thousand brochures of his teachings. His beliefs were well knit and continuous. On that account a new religion "Salmia" came into being. Salmia religion contains mainly the beliefs of Hazrat Suhail.

He used to say that he had seven principles: (1) Be attached to the book of God; (2) Follow the Sunnat of the Prophet; (3) Eat honestly earned bread; (4) Avoid causing injury (physical and mental) to others; (5) Be away from sins (6) Practice repentance; (7) Give the rights, due to others. (8) His one more saying is famous - The heart, which is empty of the knowledge of day of judgment, becomes the house, lodging the satanic desires. (9) He said also that God accepts his prayer who seeks pardon and then leans on Him.

Hazrat Suhail Tastari died in 283H/894 A.D., away from his home.

HAZRAT JUNAID ABUL QASIM BAGHDADI

He was a great Sufi, born in 298 H / 910 A.D. He lived in Baghdad. His teacher was Mohasbi, who gave him lessons even during the walks with him. Hazrat Junaid was honored as a teacher of Sufis and called Shaikh-ul-Mashaikh.

He said:

(1) If the tongue which does not keep itself busy in repeating God's praise, it is better to be dumb.

(2) If the ear that cannot hear the righteous thoughts, better be deaf.

(3) If the body which cannot serve God, better be dead.

(4) Righteousness (Khulq) is based on charity, love, good advice and patronage.

(5) Put up all Your complaints and needs before Him (God) only.

(6) Nobody can benefit or harm you without His (God's) wish.

(7) Three components of seeking pardon (from God):

  I.   Repentance

  II. Firm determination (not to do anything in future against the wishes of God)

  III. Think of the penalties of the past sins.

(8) A man who controls his ego is pious.

HAZRAT MUMSHAD ULAV DINWARI

HAZRAT MUMSHAD ULAV DINWARI - He was born in Dinwar in western Kohistan. He died in the year 299 H. He was a "Ghaus" and Qutub of his time. He got his upbringing in Baghdad. His real name was ULAV and epithet Karim Uddin. He was a rich man in the beginning, but he gave away all his riches in charity, as feeling of love of God came up intensely in his mind. Later he met Hazrat Jaseerat Basri and became his disciple. He used to wear old clothes, torn and repaired with patches. He was always busy in study of the Holy Quran and observing prayers.

His famous dictum was that "Courage is at the head of all undertakings. One whose courage is excellent, and he is truthful, and rest of his actions will be automatically good".

HAZRAT HUSAIN BIN MANSUR HALLAJ

HAZRAT HUSAIN BIN MANSUR HALLAJ - was born in Beza (Persia) in the year 244H/858 A.D. He spent early part of his life in Wasta (Iraq). He came to Baghdad in 264 H and became a disciple of Hazrat Junaid Baghdadi. He went to Holy Mecca thrice and performed Haj every time. Mansur was a weaver by profession. He often said "I am God". He was declared a heretic on this account, by Abu Daud Asfahani. In 297 H he was arrested. After one year in jail he escaped and hid himself in a place called "Sos". In 301 H he was again arrested and kept as a prisoner for 8 years in different jails. In 309 H his case was finally decided and he was condemned to death. After his death groups opined about him differently. One considered that he was a heretic and punished by death, rightly. The other group thought he was a great man and close to God and his sayings were taken in their apparent meanings and people were misguided. But they did not concentrate on the real meanings of his sayings. Maulana Rum openly praised him and believed in him. He was called a

"Martyr for Righteousness". Mansur has written many books on his own beliefs. According to Ibn Nadin, he wrote 47 books.

HAZRAT MANSUR HALLAJ said:

(1) The friendship of THE ONE, singles you out and makes you extra-ordinary.

(2) God is present in man (Hama Ost).

(3) If a man controls his ego, leaves worldly desires, he comes closer to God. In the next stage he passes the limitations of human beings and his spirit becomes one with God. Then what he intends to do, his actions do not remain his own, but they become actions of Clod.

HAZRAT ABU BAKR SHIBLI

Abu Bakr Shibli - He was a great Sufi of Maliki Sect, born in Baghdad in the year 257 H. /861 A. D. He died at the age of 87 years in Baghdad. He was a "Mohaddis" and a poet. He did not write any book but his sayings are found in different collections of books. His grave is close to that of Imam Abu Hanifa in Baghdad.

HAZRAT ABU BAKR SHIBLI said:

(1) Real worship is the one in which one does not obey the carnal self.

(2) He who has recognized God, every thing will be under his command and the person will not suffer from any grief

(3) When you are in trouble, then pray to God for relief. Hadith advised by H. Shibli.

HAZRAT ABU ALI AHMAD
BIN MOHAMMED

HAZRAT ABU ALI AHMAD BIN MOHAMMED -
Year of death 321 H / 933 A. D. He was a Sufi, a
Mohaddis and a learned man. He was a disciple of
Sheikh Habib Bhaghdadi. He was Imam of his time,
according to "Akhtar-us-Saleheen". He went to Egypt
from Baghdad and died over there. At the time of
his death he had one verse on his lips, which meant
that "I swear by you (God) that I shall continue to
see you and will not see any body else with love".

Hazrat Abu Ali Ahmad Bin Mohammed said:

(1)   One must control the eyes, tongue and ears, if
      one wants to reap full benefit, out of spiritual
      music.

(2)   According to Tazkiratul - Aulia, he said that for
      gaining Tasawuf, the Sufi should: (a) Put on
      woolen (Suf) garment; (b) Have full control over
      his ego; (c) Be away from the worldly life: (d)
      Follow the Sunnat of the Prophet.

HAZRAT ABU USMAN SAEED BIN ISLAM MAGHRIBI

Hazrart Abu Usman Saeed Bin Islam Maghribi - was a famous Sufi of his time. He died in 373 H / 983 A.D. He was a disciple of Sheikh Abul Hasan Sani, and Sheikh Abu Ali Katib. He was very rich in the beginning, but he left the worldly life on seeing the faithful life of a dog. He died in Neshapur. After 30 years of worship, he went to Holy Mecca. There he served as a Mujawir (Servant). He was spiritually benefitted there from H Abu Yaqub Nehrjuri. He then returned to Neshapur.

HAZRAT ABU USMAN SAEED said:

(1) When not all the songs of birds in the air and dance of the leaves by flow of breeze, brings you Ecstasy, know that "SAMA" has not fully developed in you spiritually.

(2) Tassavuf is leaving worldly life. Only two things guide on this path - the life of Prophet and Hadith.

(3) A Sufi is to earn his livelihood in an honest way.

(4) Do not be attached to the rich people, for help and favor, because a Derwesh, who depends on the rich people cannot get real success in his life.

HAZRAT ABUL HASAN KHIRQANI

HAZRAT ABUL HASAN KHIRQANI - Was born in 914 A.D.

He said:

(1)   If you simply move your lips whilst your heart remains unattached your prayer will not produce any effect.

(2)   None could tread one step successfully in the 'Path' without help of God.

(3)   Whom God has made ill, to him He shall play the role of a physician.

(4)   The food and drink of the Saint is remembering the names of the Lord and discourses about Him.

(5)   The greatest veil between God and man is the carnal self.

(6)   God is met when 'I' (ego) is annihilated.

(7)   Fana - to see God with thyself non-existing, "BAQA" to see God alone and not thyself, in the external existence.

(8)   A saint receives that, which is not mentioned in the scroll of destiny.

(9)   Never let a beggar turn empty handed, from the door; but give him something even if you have to contract a loan for it.

(10) If you desire to see the Master, fast every third day, then for 14 days, then for 40 days, 4 months and one year, continuously (except on days when fasting is prohibited).

HAZRAT ABU SAEED BIN KHAIRI

HAZRAT ABU SAEED BIN KHAIRI - He was born in Khurasan in 357 H / 997 A. D. His father's name was Abul Kher, who was a pharmacist. His first teacher in "Tariqat" was H. Abul Qasim Bashra Yasin. He was interested in poetry and got his disciples too interested in it. He completed his lessons in "Shafai" teachings. His other teacher was H.Abu Ali in Sarkhas. Spiritual teachings were imparted to him by Sufi Abul Fazl Mohammed bin Hasan Alsurkhi. After he returned to Mhana, he spent rest of his life in spiritual achievements and self control. He was very particular in following "Sunnat" of the Prophet. He, in later period of life, used to clean mosques, serve beggars, and help poor. He was famous for discovering the inner thoughts of his friends as well as of foes. He died in the year 440 H / 1047 A. D.

HAZRAT DATA GANJ BAKSH

HAZRAT DATA GANJ BAKSH - A great Sufi of his time, from 400 H (date of birth) to 465 H (date of death). His real name was Ali, epithet Abul Hasan and Data Ganj Baksh was his alias. He has noted in his book "Kashful Asrar" that he did not like to be addressed Data Ganj Baksh, and used to say that it was only God who can and does bestow all that He thinks proper for his servant. He is the only Giver but Data Ganj Baksh himself does not possess anything in reality that he could give to His servants. Data Sahab's ancestry goes up, by 8 generations to Hazrat Ali PBH, H Data Sahab was Khalifa of Hazrat Sheikh Abul Fazl Ghaznavi. Prince Dara Shikoh in his book "Safinatul-Aulia" has noted that Hazrat Data Ganj Baksh's home town was Ghanzi. Then his family shifted from Hajwer to Jallab which is a suburb of Ghazni and nearer to Hajwer, also a suburb of Ghazni. As such Data Sahab is remembered as Data Ganj Baksh Hajvezri, but his father is famous by the name of Hazrat Usman Jallabi. Data Sahab got his religious education in his home town from Hazrat Abul Ula. Abdul Rehman and Hazrat Abul Abbas Bin Ahmad. Hazrat Sheikh Abu Jafer Mohammed taught him the writings of Hazrat Mansur Hallaj. He visited Baghdad, Tabristan, Khurasan, Kirman, Syria, Iraq and Turkey for spiritual education, from the learned people. One day his "Pir" Hazrat Abul Fazl Ghaznavi instructed him to go to Lahore and impart spiritual teachings over there. He complied and came to Lahore along with his two associates, Hazrat Abu Samad and Hazrat Lutfi. He spent his first night at the bank of Ravi river. Next day he shifted to the place where his mausoleum exists now. He built a small mosque over there. Lately a big air-conditioned mosque has been built adjacent to his mausoleum. Data Sahab has noted in his book, "Kashful-Mahjub" that he used to keep busy in Iraq, in distribution of charity. All needy persons used to seek his help. As such he came under heavy debt. He used to worry, as to how to fulfil the needs of the needy poor. One day a Sheikh wrote to him that he should possibly fulfil the needs of others, that he can reasonably do, but should not worry for everybody, as God only, can fulfil the needs of all His servants. Data Sahab meditated at the grave of Hazrat Bayazid Bistami for 3 months, as noted in Kashul-Mahjub. Among his books are Kashul-Mahjub, Kashful-Asrar, Minhaj-Uddin and Diwan-e-Ali. Only the first two are available now.

Study of Kashful-Mahjub depicts Sayings of Data Sahib. Some sayings are his own and some are based on Hadith, sayings of Sahabas, Tabein and Taba-Tabein, which he has emphasized in the book.

Sayings of Data Sahib:

* When anybody has cut off his relations from the world he is not afraid of the people of the world.

* Data Sahib emphasized that God is not dependant upon information of the requests and needs of his Servant from him. He knows them well on His own.

* Data Sahib, emphasized that God has not left man in this world like a camel without rein, that he may do, what ever he likes. God does not force man to obey Him, nor to commit sins. Man is free in his actions, according to the capability granted by God and also the granted capability to

understand the consequences of his actions.

* Data Sahib emphasized that Repentance before God carries a priority over (routine) worship.

* When God wants to do good to His servant He makes him first conscious of his shortcomings (H).

* If one thinks that he cannot live in loneliness, he should think that Satan has taken control of his mind.

* The final result of every action by man depends on his intention (H).

* If poverty and contentment is good for the religion, it is better to be poor and contented than being wealthy.

* Data Sahib emphasized the saying that the Intention of a Momin is of greater value than his Action.

* Data Sahib emphasized the Hadith that to protect rights and duties towards ones mother is better than performing the Haj.

* I have not seen anything (in this world) which does not exhibit the greatness of God. Saying of H. Mohammad Bin Wasi emphasized by Data Sahab.

* Leaving the World cannot be a right step, till you leave your ego.

* In fact learning (Ilm) carries priority over actions(Amal), because it is only through learning that you can come closer to God.

* Miracles are true but they are dependant on the

Will of God. They show closeness of the Wali (friend of God) to God.

* If the Servant of God is contented with his duties and devotion towards Him, it is a proof that God has approved him.

* To make sacrifices for one's friend is always full of pleasure.

* One who is subservient to Wisdom becomes a Pious man and the one who follows worldly wishes, becomes mean and a heathen.

* Satan in man is his Ego itself (H).

* Miracles are allowed to Naibis (Messengers of God).

* "Fana" is that in which man (servant of God) becomes oblivious of self.

* "Baqa" is that in which man (servant of God) sees only God, nothing else.

* External Abulution is necessary for performing Namaz and Internal Abulution is necessary for MAARFAT (recognition of God).

* Repeated Repentance is permitted after repeated involvement in sins.

* True lover of God is that who is prompt to perform worship at the fixed times. Even if he is sleeping, per chance, he will get up from sleep on his own and in time.

* Love of God is a virtue found in the heart of an obedient Momin.

* Data Sahib emphasized that real Love is not lessened by cruelty (by the beloved towards him)

nor it is increased by obligations and gifts to him (Yahya Bin Maaz Razi).

* In all dealings Ethics is a very good thing.

* In all dealings three things are noble, among Muslim brotherhood: (a) To wish him when you meet; (b) To accommodate him in a seat, in a gathering; (c) To address him with good epithets-H.

* Putting up Pleas is a Stranger's behavior and is a cruelty towards one's own associate.

* Satan is an associate of man when he is lonely (H).

* One should not eat much, nor worry about food day and night.

* One should sleep, only when he is feeling intensely sleepy.

* Do not walk ahead of your group. It shows vanity.

* If one has a right point, then Speech is better than silence, but if one is on the wrong, then silence is better than speech.

* If one makes request to God through an intermediary person, but he is mentally dependant on God's wish, then he is nearer to God in his obedience.

* There is no greater harmful action than freedom of libido.

* There are three types of Beliefs: (a) Belief on acquiring knowledge (Ilm-ul-Yaqeen); (b) Belief on seeing (Ain-ul-Yaqeen); (c) Final belief on deduction after seeing (Haq-ul-Yaqeen)

* It is a miracle of the Holy Quran that one does not feel uneasy (bored) on listening or reading it.

* Both Animals and Men enjoy good music.

* Spirit is a nicety and so is Music. Hence, they are attracted towards each other.

* Do not listen (devotional) music, unless you need it and do not make a habit of it.

HAZRAT IMAM GHIZALI

Hazrat Imam Ghizali - He was born in 445 H in the district of Tehran of Khurasan. His father was a cotton seller. His family name came to be known as Ghizali, which in Arabic means Cotton seller. He got training from the great learned man, Allama Abu Ishaq Shirazi, till the teacher died. He later reached the Durbar of Nizam-ul-Mulk at Neshapur and was greatly honored. He was made a high officer of Madarasa-e-Nizami at the early age of 34. There were 300 students and one hundred nobles who attended his intellectual discourses, which have been preserved in "Majlis Ghizali", by his disciples. In 488 H Ghizali left Baghdad as a Sufi and went to Damascus and busied himself in the worship of God. From there he went to Jerusalem, and for Haj. He visited Alexandria as well. Al Ghizali entered the field of Sufism, when there was a strong protest against formation of Orthodox Islam, which placed great emphasis on the external duties and enforced strict and rigid beliefs. Hazrat Farid Uddin Attar and after him Hazrat Jalal Uddin Rumi drew copiously from

Al Ghazali and made rich pages of Persian Sufi Literature.

Though Imam Ghizali resolved not to go to King's court, he was persuaded in 499 Hirji by Saljuqi King, and again started teaching at Madarsa-e-Nizamia at Neshapur. After the King's death in 500 H. Ghizali again went back to solitude. Ghizali was keen to learn Ahadith. He got an opportunity to get teaching from the famous Mohaddis Hafiz Umar bin Abi Hasan Tus, Mohaddis of his time. He was entertained as a guest in Ghazali's house. Imam Ghazali lived only for 55 years. He imparted knowledge to his students, whose number was never less than 150. He has written many books on Philosophy and Religion. It is said that average of his writings was 16 pages every day, considering the span of his life. His famous book is Ahya-ul Uloom. He died in 505 H at Tehran and is buried there.

Hazrat Al Ghazali Said:

The only course for enlightenment of the Sufi is when the hour arrives for spiritual illumination.

HAZRAT SHEIKH ABDUL QADIR JEELANI

HAZRAT SHEIKH ABDUL QADIR JEELANI, bin Saleh Abdullah bin Jangi Dost - He was the originator of Qadaria Sufi Sect. he was a learned· follower of Imam Hanmbali as well. He was born in 470 H/ 1077-78 A.D. and died in 560 H/1160 A.D. His birth was at Neef, District Jeelan. He went to Baghdad at the age of 18 for education and remained there until his death. Among his teachers were Hazrat Abul Wafa bin Aqeel, Hazrat Abu Saad Mubarik

Mukharami, Hazrat Abu Mohammed Jafar Siraj and Hazrat Abul Kher Hammad. At the age of 50 he gave his first oration (Religious) on 521 H / 1127 A.D. It was very much appreciated far and wide. The Madarsa (School) of his teacher Mukharami was entrusted to him, which was aided by the rich financially and served physically by the poor. It is said that many Christians and Jews adopted Islam after hearing his beautiful and impressive religious orations. Hazrat Abdul Qadir was unconcerned with worldly needs and was fearless in speaking truth from his childhood. He was helpful to poor. During his life time Sufism made great progress. A century earlier, it was disputed whether one should adopt Sufi cult, which confronted Shariat at times. Sheikh guided as to how Sufism (Tariqat) and Shariat can go together hand in hand. Sheikh's teacher Hazrat Abu Aqeel and some conservative Hanmbalis were against Sufism. Among Sheikh's writings were "Algani-tul-Talibeen, Tareequl-haq and Futuh-ul-Ghaib, which discuss Hanmbalism and Sufism. Fateh-Rabbani and Fez-e-Rabbani contain 78 orations of Sheikh. They had been compiled by Sheikh's grandson Sh. Afif Uddin Mubarik. There is a collection of his letters as well in which the secrets of Marfat and Tariqat are discussed. Sheikh's mausoleum is in Baghdad and is visited by lacs of people every year. Sheikh married 4 times, but had only one wife at a time.

Sheikh emphasized not to be soft on the matters of Shariat, though he practiced Tariqat as well.

He further advised that -

Renunciation of this world, not out of self's desire (ego), nor by the force of one's circumstances, but just to fulfil the commandment of God, puts a man in a proper situation to establish contact with, and talk to the world.

Protect your heart for not leaning towards what you have renounced, your past desires, wishes & efforts in that direction.

Protect your heart from loosing patience, establish harmony & pleasure with God, at the time when calamity befalls you.

HAZRAT SHEIKH FARID UDDIN ATTAR

HAZRAT SHEIKH FARID UDDIN ATTAR - was a famous Sufi poet in the middle of 6th. century Hijri. He was born at Neshapur and died in 1326 A. D. He spent his youth in pursuit of learning. Maulana Rum was greatly benefitted by the teachings of Sh. Farid Uddin Attar. He travelled to Egypt, Damascus, India, Turkey, and the Holy Mecca. He was a Pharmacist by profession. One day a Derwesh, came to him and rested near the door step of his house. Hazrat Attar asked him as to what he wanted? He replied "Care for yourself. There is no stability in life. See what is life". Saying this he laid himself down and died. The Sheikh was very much affected by this incidence and immediately left his shop, in search of spiritual men. The Sheikh wrote three books which are very well known. His Odes (Qasida) and poetry comprise ten thousand verses, Tazakaratul-Aulia is the second book and the third is a Mathnavi.

Hazrat Sh. Farid Uddin Attar said:

(1) A Sufi's journey is through seven valleys; (a) Quest-Talab-SALIK' (b) LOVE-ISHQ; (c)KNOWLEDGE-Marfat, God is seen in all; (d) DETACHMENT-fiqr; (e) UNITY Tauheed, Ecstasy & vision, (f) AMAZEMENT - Hayrut; (g) ANNIHILATION OF SELF-Fana.

(2) Every atom in the Universe is whirling with madness of love and its birth too is through love.

(3) Desire to accumulate good, alone, shall accompany one to the other world. It developes and above all remembrance of Death comes to the forefront in one's life.

(4) Great Saints are ever living.

(5) TAWANGER-e-SHAKIR and FAQIR-e-SABIR are two great qualities.

HAZRAT MOIN UDDIN CHISTI

HAZRAT KHWAJA MOIN UDDIN CHISTI - From 536 H / 1141 A. D. to 633 H / 1236 A.D. He was a famous Sufi saint of the Indian subcontinent. He was the originator of Chistia sect in India. He was born in Saryar - a town in Seestan. His father Hazrat Ghias Uddin Hasan was a very wealthy merchant, but at the same time a very pious man. His ancestry reaches up to Hazrat Ali from both paternal and maternal side. When his father died, Kh. Moin

Uddin was 20 years in age. He had left a garden and a flour mill (Chakki) in inheritance. Thereupon Kh. Sahab took up the profession of gardening in the beginning, doing labor himself. One day while he was resting in his garden, a Sufi - Hazrat Ibrahim Qalander who was a "Majzub" visited him in his garden. Khwaja sahab was so much influenced and impressed on meeting him that he started taking keen interest in Sufism. He gave away all his belongings in charity and left for Samarqand and Bukhara, which were centers of Islamic education in those days. There, he received education from the learned persons. On way to Iraq he passed through the town of Harwn in Dist. Neshapur. There he met Khwaja Usman Harwani and became his disciple. He remained with his teacher on his extensive travels and imbibed his spiritual guidance. Thereafter he himself traveled to other Islamic centers. He met during this period Sheikh Abdul Qadir Jeelani, Hazrat Abdul Qadir Suharwardi, Sh. Abu Saeed Tabrezi and Sh. Abdul Wahid Ghaznavi. Later he came to India and remained for a period in Lahore and he spent his time in meditation at the grave of Hazrat Ali Hajweri (Data Sahab). Later he went to Ajmere and from there spread the message of Islam and got married there. According to Sh. Abdul Haq Mohaddis Dehlvi one of his marriages was with the daughter of a Hindu Raja. He died in Ajmere and his mausoleum is visited by a large number of Hindus and Muslims every year. He had three sons and a daughter named Bibi Jamal. His mausoleum was constructed, on the order of a Khilji King. Mohammed bin Tughlaq is known to have visited his shrine, and during the reign of Akbar, his mausoleum had become famous, as the greatest one in the subcontinent. Khwaja Sahab was a great pious man and Islam spread far and wide by his teachings. He visited Delhi twice, but kept himself aloof from the center of politics. He introduced the social revolution silently. He is said to have written many books, out of which "Kashf-ulMahjoob" and "Anis-ul-Arwah" are famous. Among his Khalifas were Hazrat Kh. Qutub Uddin Bakhtayar Kaki, Hazrat Hameed Uddin Nagori, Bibi Hafiza Jamal, Sultan Masud Ghazi, Sh Wajeeh Uddin, Sh. Waheed Uddin. He was very compassionate to others.

According to him, (1) True religion is service of the Creation (Khalq); (2) One should be charitable like the river, warm like the sun, and entertaining to men like the Earth.

Names of prominent Sufis of Chistia Sect, who followed Hazrat Kh. Moin Uddin Chisti, are noted below in an order that shows Succession or Khilaat.

Hazrat Moin Uddin Chisti

536H/1 161 A.D. to 633H/1236 A.D.5

Hazrat Qutub Uddin Bakhtiyar Kaki 583H/1107 A.D. to 63211/1235 A.D.	Hazrat Harneed Uddin Nagori 642H/1244 A.D
Baba Farid Uddin Ganj Shakr 584H/1180 A.D. to 66411/1265 A.D	Hazrat Badr Uddin Ghaznavi
Hazrat Nizam Uddin Aulia 636H to 726H/1325 A.D. t	Hazrat Ala Uddin Sabir Kalyari Born in 592H.
Haarat Naoir Uddin Chirag Delhi 768EI/1362A.D. (year of death	Hazrat Burhan Uddin Ghareeb 654H/1256 A.D. to738H/1337 A.D.
Hazrat Syed Mohammad Al Husaini Gesudaraz 721H to 825H/1422 A.D.	Hazrat Allarna Karnal Uddin

HAZRAT LAL SHAHBAZ QALANDER

HAZRAT LAL SHAHBAZ QALANDER - He was a great Sindhi Sufi Saint of Suharwardia order and a great Persian poet. He was born in 538H /1144 A.D. at Marwan. Marwand is a place situated close to Herat in Afghanistan. He died at the age of 95 years, on the 21st Shaban in 633/1236 A.D., at Sehwan Sharif in Sindh. He is buried over there. His father's name was Hazrat Hassan Kabeer-Uddin. His mother was the daughter of Syed Sultan Shah ruler of Marwand. The real name of Hazrat Lal Shahbaz Qalander was Hazrat Sheikh Uthman Marwandi. As he was born in Marwand, Marwandi is suffixed to his name. He came to be known popularly by the name Hazrat Lal Shahbaz Qalander. Lal denoted his red dress, which he always wore. Shahbaz means Royal Falcon, which symbolised his eminent place in spirituality. Qalander stood for self-detatchment from worldly affairs and commitment to the contemplation of divinity.

Hazrat Lal Shahbaz Qalander became a Hafiz of the Holy Quran (memorised the Holy Quran) at the young age of seven years. He learned Persian and Arabic languages. His first spiritual teacher was Baba Ibrahim, he expressed his desire to be intiated to Qalandaria Sect. He remained with Baba for one year. He was awarded the mantle of the order (Kharqa). Later he came across Hazrat Sheikh-al-Islam Baha-Uddin Zakaria of Multan. He came to be considered as a close spiritual friend of the Sheikh. He came in contact with other great contemporary Sufis, like Hazrat Baba Farid Uddin Masood Ganj

Shakar, Hazrat Makhdoom Jahanian Jehan Gasht, and Hazrat Boo Ali Qlanader of Panipat.

Hazrat Lal Shahbaz Qalander traveled widely to places like Baghdad, Balakh, Bukhara, Madina Sharif, Ajodhan (Pak Pattan Sharif, where Hazrat Baba Farid-Uddin Masood resided). He visited Samarqand and Thatta Nager. Finally he came to Panipat and came across Hazrat Bu Ali Qalander, who was of the same Qalandaria Sect. He advised him to go to Sindh and preach Islam there. He came to Multan where Mohammad Khan (Shaheed) son of Sultan Ghias Uddin Balban was the Ruler. He held Hazrat Lal Shahbaz Qalander in great esteem. A shrine was constructed by the order of the ruler in Multan. But Hazrat Lal Shahbaz Qalander proceded to his final destination Sehwan Sharif, in Sindh. An Urs is held every year in the month of Shaban, the month in which he died. A great number of Muslims and Hindus visit the shrine to pay homage to him. A popular Sindhi song starting with the words "Jhule Lalan Rakheo Bala...." is sung in his honor in high beat both by Hindus and Muslims at the time of Urs and otherwise too at many places in North India and Pakistan. There is a spring in Sehwan Sharif, where people suffering from skin disease gather and are cured of the ailments by bathing in the spring.

Hazrat Lal Shahbaz Qalander was a great Persian Poet. According to Burton "He was a linguistic and a grammarian. He wrote certain books which are taught in Maktabs. These were Uqd, Kism, Doyum, Djnas and Mezam Sharif." The above observations of Burton have been quoted by Dr. Sadarangani in his book, "Persian Poets of Sind" and by the writer of Gazeteer, Vol. A page 94 and by Sheikh M. Mohammad Ikram, the author of Muaj c Kauser and

by Fateh Mohammad Sehwani in his Qalandarnama.
Hazrat Lal Shabaz Qalander was friendly with the
contemporary Sufi saints, like Hazrat Farid Uddin
Masood Ganj Shakar, Hazrat Syed Jalal Bukhari,
Hazrat Sheikh Baha Uddin Zakaria of Multan, of the
same Suharwardi order. It is said that he along with
the above three Sufis observed Chilla (40 days
seclusion) in Sehwan Sharif, in a house with pillars.

HAZRAT QUTUB UDDIN BAKATIAR KAKI

HAZRAT QUTUB UDDIN BAKHTIAR KAKI -
From 583 H / 1187 A. D. to 633 H / 1235 A. D. His
father's name was Syed Kamal Uddin and his
ancestery is traced back to Hazrath Syedna Imam
Hasan P.B.H. He was a famous Sufi saint. He was
born in "Osh". He was one and a half years old when
his father died and he was brought up under the
supervision of his mother. At the age of 5 years he
started education under Maulana Abdul Hafis, who
was a pious man. He educated him, both in worldly
and spiritual teachings. When Khwaja Moin Uddin
Chisti came to Osh, Hazrat Qutub Uddin became his
disciple. At that time he was 17 years old. He was
given "Khilafat" by Khwaja Moin Uddin. Hazrat Kaki
in his writings has noted about his travels and
meetings with the learned Sheikhs. In Baghdad he
met Sh. Shahab Uddin Suhrwardi, Sh. Wahid Uddin
Kirmani. Kh. Abu Yusuf Chisti, Hazrat Abul Lais
Samarqandi, Sh. Burhan Uddin Chisti and Sh.
Mohammed Asfahani. He came to know in Baghdad
that Kh Moin Uddin was going to India. There upon

he too started (in his company)for India. During the journey he met Hazrat Bahauddun Zakaria at Multan. On reaching India Khwaja Sahib asked him to be stationed at Delhi.

On reaching Delhi he was welcomed by Sultan Shamsuddin Altamas. The Sultan used to meet him twice a week, as long as Kh. Kaki stayed in Kelo-Khar near Delhi. On repeated requests of the Sultan, he came to stay in Delhi proper. There he received love and appreciation of the residents of Delhi. He was a very contented person. In spite of the Sultan being his disciple, he often used to be without food in his house. At times in such a situation, he got some food on loan from a neighbour.

One day the neighbour taunted that if she would not extend that courtesy, H.Kh. Kaki's children would die of hunger. When he came to know about this remark, of the neighbor, he directed that no loan be taken from her and that "Kak" (a biscuit type of bread) be taken out, when needed, from the mantle shelf of his prayer room "Hujra".That is the reason that he got the epithet "Kaki".

He was very fond of "Sama" (Qawwali). On one occasion on hearing a verse during Sama, he became unconscious and remained in that condition for 7 days. On another occasion, Hazrat Qutub Uddin Kaki on hearing another verse, became unconscious for three days and died in that condition. He has written one book.

"Fawaid ul Saleheen". His other book contains his own poetry. His famous disciples were Sh. Farid Uddin Ganj Shakar, Sultan Shams Uddin Altamash, Qazi Hameed Uddin Nagori, besides many others.

He is buried about 11 miles from Delhi proper (old) in Mehroli-usually called"Qutub Sahab".

Khwaja Qutub Uddin Kaki's sayings:

(1)   A man reaches the zenith of his achievement in observing four things: (a) Sleeps less; (b) Eats less; (c) Talks less; (d) Attaches himself less with worldly people.

(2)   Unless one enters Sufism with heart, he is not on the right path and will not reach his goal.

HAZRAT BABA FARID GANJ SHAKAR

Hazrat Farid Uddin Ganj Shakar - Was a famous Sufi saint of the subcontinent of Chistia sect. His real name was Farid Uddin Alias Masood, Epiteth Ganj Shaker. Hisfather's name was Jamal Uddin, who was son of Hazrat Qazi Shoab. He came to Qasur (in Pakistan now) from Kabul during the attack of Changiz Khan. There is some difference of opinion regarding the date of birth of Baba Farid, In Searat-ul-Aulia, it is noted 569 H 173-74 A.D., but in the history of Farishta it is mentioned 584 H/1 180 A. D. Baba Farid is addressed as Ganj Shakar on the basis of a few anecdotes. One is that he was way fond of sugar. The other is that his mother to encourage the young boy used to put a small amount of sugar under his prayer mat, saying, this was a gift from Allah to those who were steadfast in their prayers. As it happened one day she forgot to place the sugar as per her routine, yet he found, to her surprise, sugar under the prayer mat. To her querry of who as to who had given it to him, he replied that Allah, as usual put sugar under the prayer mat. Another anecdote goes that one day a caravan carrying bags of sugar on camels passed nearby. Baba Farid inquired about the contents of the bags and the caravan men replied it contained salt. On reaching their destination when they checked their bags they were astounded to find them all full of salt. They repented and retraced their steps to Baba Farid and most humbly sought his pardon and forgiveness. Baba Farid in his grace and mercy granted them. On their return to their caravan they found that miraculously the salt bags were reconverted to sugar. It was a miracle of Baba Farid.

Baba Farid's ancestry goes up to Hazrat Umar Faruq. At an early age he became a Hafiz of the Quran and at the age of 18 he went to Multan, a center of learning of the subcontinent, for further education. He studied "Fiqah" from Maulana Minhaj Uddin Tirmezi. There he met Hazrat Kh. Bakhtiar Kaki and became his disciple. For further education he traveled to Qandhar, Baghdad, Badakhshan and Bukhara. During this journey he performed Haj as well. He was greatly benefitted by many Sheikhs. Out of them were Hazrat Shahab Uddin Suharwardi, Hazrat Farid Uddin Attar, Hazrat Baha Uddin Zakaria and Khwaja Kaki. He was given Khilafat by H.Kh. Kaki. He started residing in a room near Ghaznavi Gate. It was during that period that he met H.Kh. Moin Uddin Chisti, and he too gave him "Khilfat". At the instruction of his Sheikh, he went to Hansi. On the death of H.Kh. Bakhtiar Kaki he came back to Delhi, and according to latter's will was gifted by Qazi Hameed Uddin Nagoria, a dress and other articles left for him by his Sheikh. Then he returned to his home town to meet his mother. After that he started preaching, (to spread Islam), in a village called Ajodhan, which later on came to be known as Pak Pattan, at the instance of Emperor Akbar. During his stay at Ajodhan, Sultan Nasir Uddin Mahmud, visited him. Then the Sultan sent his commander Ghias Uddin Balban, with an endowment of 4 villages and cash. Hazrat Baba Farid accepted the cash, which he distributed amongst the poor, but declined to accept the grant of landed property. Later on Baba Farid married the daughter of Ghias Uddin Balban. On the death of Baba Farid, Balban got the mausoleum constructed, under the supervision of H. Kh. Nizam Uddin Aulia. His year of death, as recorded in "Ser-ulAulia" is 664 H. Many Rajput tribes, such as Sial and Watto got converted to Islam, on Baba's preaching. Skeikh Abdul Haq Mohaddis Dehlvi, has noted in "Akhbar-ul-Akhyar" that Baba Farid was not only a great Khalifa of Hazrat Bakhtiar Kaki, but was directly connected with Kh. Moin Uddin Chisti Ajmeri, as well. Among Baba Farid's Khulafa, were Hazrat Nizam Uddin Aulia, Kh. Ala Uddin Ali Sabir Kalyari. H. Sh. Jamal Uddin of Hansi. Chistia Sect was introduced by Kh. Moin Uddin Chisti, but it was spread by Baba Farid, as such he is called, Adam - the second of Chistia sect. He could not write his own book ,as he spent most of his time in collecting the teachings of his teacher, H.Kh. Bakhtiar Kaki, which were compiled in a book. His own teachings and sayings were compiled by his disciple Kh. Nizam Uddin Aulia in his book "Rahat-ul-Qulub". They are also to be found in "Seratul-Aulia". The famous historian and traveller Ibn Babuta visited the mausoleum of Baba Farid and met his grandson Sh. Alauddin.

Baba's teachings are noted in Guru Granth Sahab,

the Holy book of Sikhs and read over and over again in their prayers.

Sayings of Baba Farid:

(1) Try to be kind to your enemies as far as possible.

(2) Clear your debt as early as possible.

(3) Do not abandon your good work on the cold remarks of others.

(4) Disappointment is (sometimes) an occasion for the progress (in life).

(5) The wish to remain free and unoccupied with pursuits in life is a sign of weakness.

(6) Sufi is one who cleanses every thing, but is not spoiled himself.

(7) Depict yourself as you really happen to be, otherwise the reality will itself open (someday).

(8) Do not consider a fool as living (active).

(9) Do not sell anything which cannot be purchased

(10) Do not partake every body's bread, but give your bread to everyone.

(11) Do not be proud of your misdoings (sins).

(12) Do not run after self decorations.

(13) Do not abandon your endeavors in life.

(14) Be always cautious of the person who is afraid of you.

(15) Immediately cut off your relations totally with your enemy, whose bad intentions you have discovered by your intuition.

(16) Leave that righteousness which appears False. Some people speak truth, in such a way that it appears untrue.

(17) Keep away from a fool who depicts himself as Wise.

(18) Keep your inner self better than your exterior.

(19) Do not forget your religion if you sit in the company of the wealthy people.

(20) There is no return of the (past) time.

(21) Learn art, even if you have to take a lowly position (to start it).

(22) The malice of an enemy is broken down, when you consult him (sincerely).

(23) Do not be frustrated if any misfortune befalls you from God.

(24) The pleasure in life comes in if you do not get disappointed on not getting anything (you want), but take a care-free attitude.

(25) Sufi will die of hunger but will not borrow for the pleasure of his ego, because incurring debt and contentment are poles apart.

(26) Sometimes, discussion between two persons on a subject is better than one's thinking over it for 2 years himself.

(27) Do not show off your virtues and keep hidden Your vices.

(28) Do good deeds that people may consider you alive (in their mind) even when you are dead.

(29) Those who feed birds, may get "Huma" some

day. (Huma is a mythological bird. If it passes over somebody's head he gets kingship sooner or later.)

(30) If somebody is enlightened with the secrets of the universe, he leaves worldly thoughts and pursuits.

(31) If anybody is Prime in his specialty, he remains drowned in its thoughts.

(32) Everything happens according to the Wish of God.

(33) Sometimes spiritual men are found in the dress of ordinary men.

(34) Treat everybody with courtesy. Do not consider anybody bad in dealings. Keep in mind your own drawbacks.

(35) Sale of Sufi-type (darweshaha) is that in which any cost given by the purchaser is accepted and the material is not demanded back.

HAZRAT SHEIKH BAHA UDDIN ZAKARIA

HAZRAT SHEIKH BAHA UDDIN ZAKARIA - Born 578 H / 1182 A. D. and died in 661 H / 1262 A. D. He belonged to Suharwardi Sect of Sufis and was a great Sufi of India. His Father's name was Hazrat Wajeeh Uddin Mohammed. He was born at Kot Karoor District of Muzzaffer Garh. There are different opinions regarding years of his birth and death. At the age of seven he learned the Holy Quaran by heart. His father died when Hazrat Zakaria was 12 years of age. He went to Bukhara, Khurasan, Medina and Palestine and other centers of learning. During his stay in Medina he learned Hadith from Mohaddis Sheikh Kamal Uddin. He then went to Jerusalem and Baghdad and became disciple of Sheikh Shahab Uddin Suhrwardi. He gave him certificate of Khilafat and asked him to go to Multan and benefit people over there. He stayed in Multan for 50 years. His Khanqah is a beautiful building and was the center of learning in India during Medieval period. Sultan Shamsuddin Altamash gave him the post of "Sheikh-ul-Islam" which continued after his death, in his family, for some period of time. His disciples are mostly limited to Sindh, Punjab and some to Hirat, Hamadan and Bukhara. His system of Sufism was different from Chistia sect. He was very friendly with Sheikh Farid Uddin Ganj Shakar, who repeated his principles as basis of piety. Sheikh Zakaria was a rich man through Agriculture and Trade. He used to feed the needy and poor in hundred. His own diet was limited. His one famous miracle is, that he saved a drowning boat in river Chenab, The boat men of that place still loudly repeat his name, when sailing. He was not against having relations with Kings and officers. He is buried in a beautiful Mausoleum in Multan, which he himself is supposed to have constructed. He had seven sons and his famous disciple was Syed Usman alias Lalbaz Sindhi.

His principles were: (1) Firstly know this world and do not be disheartened; (2) Secondly serve the progeny and consider their rights; (3) Desire good life after death and make efforts for it. He once wrote to his disciple: (a) That safety of the body lies in eating a little; (b) Safety of spirituality lies in not committing sins; (c) Safety of religion lies in observing prayers; (4) He further used to say that World is nothing before the eyes of a Darwesh (Monk). He is neither sad on loosing anything, nor happy on gaining anything; (5) Sufism involves keeping secrets of the Universe and not donning only the 5ufi dress.

HAZRAT SABIR KALYARI

HAZRAT SABIR KALYARI - His real name was Alauddin Ahmad, alias Makhdoom Sabir. His ancestry goes up to Ghaus-e-Azam Abdul Qadir Jeelani. He was born in 592 H and died in Piran Kalyar in District Saharanpur (U.P. India). His mother was sister of Baba Farid Ganj Shakar, who gave him spiritual education. He remained with his uncle for 12 years and completed worldly and spiritual education. He was a very pious man and used to keep fasts very often. He remained bare footed and passed time in solitude. In 625 H Baba Farid gave him "Khilafat" and on his direction he went to Kalyar Sharif, a lonely place and stayed there through out. Khwaja Shams Uddin Turk was his Khalifa and successor, who founded Chistia-Sabiria sect of Sufism.

HAZRAT MAULANA JALAL UDDIN RUMI

HAZRAT MAULANA JALAL UDDIN RUMI - From 1207 to 1272 A. D. His father's name was M. Baha Uddin, who was a learned man. He had some differences with Ala Uddin Mohammed, Kharzan Shah, so he left the place and came to Neshapur. Maulana Rum, who was born in Balakh, was only a child, when his father shifted to Neshapur. His father met a Sufi saint Sheikh Farid Uddin Attar there, who blessed Rumi on taking him in his lap M.Rumi's father then brought him to Konia, a city in Asia minor and settled there. M. Rumi first became a disciple of Sheikh Burhan Uddin Terrnizi and then another saint Shams Tabrez. Hazrat Shams Tabrez left Konia on getting fed up of the sons of his disciple Maulana Rum. Maulana's poetry is based on his sentiments on the separation from his mentor H Shams Tabrez. Maulana's poetry depicts TASSAWUF in his Mathnavi, which is called the (Holy) Quran in Persian language. He has depicted it with stories and lessons, derived from them.

His saying mainly from his famous Mathnavi are:

- God guides one who directs himself towards Him.

- One who comes forward towards Me (God), by the breadth of a hand, I shall come near him 4 times of that distance. -H.

- One who comes forward towards Me (God) walking, I shall come running near him. -H.

- The Prophet PBH declared that there is no real friend of mine, except God. -H.

- In the beginning, Momin desires heaven, but after devotion and observation, only the intense desire to see God remains. God the Great on seeing his capability, bestows him Heaven.

- Be kind to servants.

- True believers of God do not hesitate in nursing the patients.

- Be cautious of the foresight of a Momin, because he sees everything in the light from God.

- As a man is a viceroy of God on Earth, he is therefore, the Center and an essence of existing Universe.

- The physical eye cannot see, the full reality of anything.

- The body of man is moved by the spirit, but it is regretted that man is after nourishing the body and not the Spirit.

- When fruit is unripe, it is firmly attached to a branch of the tree and is hard to pluck it.

- The personality of a man is a collection of many personalities. It is like a deep sea.

- A glimpse of light of God, finishes human weakness.

- To sit by the side of a beloved and read her letters is a cause for her anger. The Lover forgets everything and gets engrossed in getting a view of the beloved.

- The temporary beauty is not worth living for. Love should be with the spirit which is everlasting.

- Youth is like cash in the body. The love is for the cash and not for the container.

- Search is a sign of reaching the goal.

- Sometimes Love is hidden in Cruelty and at another Cruelty is hidden in love.

- On reaching the stage of certainty, the flight of the Spirit is extremely simple. Man does not stumble at all.

- Those who have no knowledge to the level of certainty, they are the ones who are affected by the rumors.

- It is easy for a man to perform a work, for which he is created.

- I recognized God by the changes in my determination. Hazrat Ali's saying emphasised by Maulana Rum.

- You must fulfil your promises.

- A man is as old as his knowledge.

- Patience changes troubles into comfort.

- I, (God), do the same thing as my Servant, thinks about me.- Emphasised by Maulana Rum.

- Man forgets his grief in the excitement of love.

- It is a real attainment that the man continues to pray and also be contented on God's wishes

- Anything received from the Beloved is good.

- Every man's pleasure is at His, God's order.

- The verses of the Holy Quoran carry many meanings.

- I do not want anything for self, but because it is at the order of God.

- My belief is for the approval of God, not for the greed of Heaven.

- My hatred towards sin is also for the approval by God, but not out of fear of Hell.

- The Prophet addressed the Ummat, that I am behind YOU like a Father. -H.

- Your love for a spiritual man is due to the effect of his Love for you.

- If a man becomes free from raising objections and reasoning, he can become secret-holder of God.

- Inner dirt is washed away by tears.

- God is the source of all virtues in man. If man thinks it, to be a source a from created beings, it is his bad luck.

- The worldly Love is a bridge for the Real Love (the Love of God).

- To offer prayer is a sacrifice of Ego.

- On concentratina on God. one can be free from Libido and Greed.

- When all the resources of the world are finished, then man turns toward God.

- It is a saying of the Prophet that what an ignorant man is obliged to do, is performed by an intelligent man at an early stage of work.

- It is lack of knowledge of man, that he feels dismal, on imaginary griefs. In search for life they acquire death.

- The kindness of God seeks occasions to do kindness to man.

- Whatever you cannot attain by your own efforts, will be attainable by the good wishes of the man of God (spiritual Man).

- God says that He observes the real intention of man (Hadith). Emphasised by Maulana.

- The only way to clean your heart, is to keep yourself away from the worldly desires.

- All the worldly things intoxicate man and work like alcohol, which if one does not get, one feels pain.

- Efforts and Search lead you to success.

- In the heart of every follower, the promise of the day of Creation resounds. On that account the worldly troubles get milder.

- Man thanks God sometimes, but complains most of the time.

- With high Spiritual attainment, all the secrets open to you.

- My contentment is my Prayer.

- God conceals the faults of men, but the non-believer exhibits their faults.

- In the heat of revenge - the murderer confesses his guilt.

- Fiery temper is a part of the Hell.

- Prayer for Forgiveness changes the nature of the act. The sins are converted into virtues.

- Ego killed intelligence and became Lord, though it was a servant.

- You will get spiritual nourishment, when you keep your stomach empty.

- The benefit that you get from the bread, is bestowed only by God. You can get the benefit bestowed on you without the bread.

- The ego, like a dog in his house, is like a Lion. Intelligence wanders (on this situation).

- Effect of foolishness is a curse from God. In no way you can ward it off, by any plan.

- Make friends with the intelligent people, on the basis of their knowledge.

- God will praise man's sacrifice in such a way that the Universe will envy it.

- Unworthy men, many a times, get wealthy, but they do not appreciate it.

- To criticize the decisions of God is useless. His every act is appropriate.

- Satan misguides conscience as such man is deprived from getting the nectar of immortaility (Ab-e-hyat).

- Man can understand the reality, if he has intelligence and sense of Justice.

- One who will keep away himself from the Satanic pleasures will get reward in Heaven.

- When man is relieved of his troubles, he reverts

to the vices as before.

- God is pleased with his grateful servants.

- For every sickness brought on Earth by God, He brought its cure.

- Many matters appear difficult in the beginning, but become easier later on.

- Spirit is not limited by time and space as such there is no old age or tiredness for it.

- One who has not tasted it (a thing). does not know about it.

- If you will be firm to mean people they will be obedient to you.

- Mean persons work well with harsh people, but are cruel to the noble men.

- The purpose for creation of man and Jin, is worship of God and obedience.

- Wealthy people are strong headed.

- Mouse is afraid of a cat, not of a lion.

- Hunger is approved by Spiritual persons. Pain and grief is the food of Lovers.

- One who prays with devotion and a clean heart will discover Reality.

- Sea debars the fishes to go out and the land animals to come in.

- If you want Freedom and Life in your heart, then pray to God and be obedient.

- If you thank God, He will give you more.

- If a man does not like any thing for himself, there may be betterment for him in that dislike.

- See Laila with the eyes of Majnun.

- Love first entangles one, then makes him restless.

- Nothing is bad in this world by itself, it is bad in relation to something.

- A man who does not show mercy to others will not be shown mercy by God.

- Any disagreeable thought becomes a catalyst for achieving an agreeable thing. It then becomes an agreeable thought.

- If a man cannot perform sacrificial efforts himself, he should show patience on the troubles. They become replacement for his sacrificial acts.

- Dirty things are also necessary in this world, but they cannot be considered clean on that account.

- God ordinarily covers the faults in the first instance but catches the person in repeating them again and again.

- When any body, who has fallen himself in the fireplace, it is foolishness to inquire him about his condition.

- When the greatness of God's commandment does not suit their understanding they feel uncomfortable and the advice becomes boredom to them.

- God made creation in darkness at first, then brought it into light.

- Man should copy the methods of asking pardon of God from his Father Adam.

- To take an examination of the beloved is not expected of the lover.

- To try God is a disrespect towards Him. It can become a cause for one's own destruction.

- Abu Jehl asked H Mohammed PBH for the miracle of Splitting of moon so he suffered ultimately.

- If a man gives up the enjoyment of the worldly pleasure then giving up itself becomes pleasure for him.

- If God had not planned creation of man, the universe would not have been there.

- A house for self, and getting fruits from the trees, came into being, but their plans came into the mind before their physical appearance.

- The sun is triveal in comparison to the light of Reality.

- Flame appears darker before the light of God.

- It is a deception of thinking that the worldly things are costly though they are worthless in reality.

- He is the real man who recognizes the Creator and keeps his ego under control.

- When God wants to destroy any person, every particle of the universe becomes his enemy.

- If it is wrong to search for a camel on a rooftop it is also wrong to search for God from the throne and under the Crown. Emphasised by Maulana Rumi.

- Although man was evolved from lifeless stage he

refuses to recoanize the day of Judgement.

- When water is available one does away with dry ablution (Tayyamum).

- God puts man to tests and brings to light his virtues.

- Example of a worldly man is like that of a dog who leaves good game and rushes towards beggars and the poor for food.

- Great people too have gone to dust by the curses and revenge of beggars.

- Sinners are necessary in the management of Nature.

- To progress to the higher stages, by sticking to one's religion, creates solidity in his belief.

- Nobody can loose himself.

- Chains are of two types: one of fear and the other of love.

- Man's greed makes his bad deeds appear good to him, just as fire makes a tinder appear beautiful.

- When a man dies all his activities are stopped but three things remain, charity without object of gain, imparted knowledge which benefits others and noble progeny who should pray for his soul

- It is not easy to deceive the spiritual people.

- Man's worldly desires come out of his greed. He thinks worldly matters as wisdom only. Intelligence can be defeated by the desires of man.

- Man should give up remorse, take to good deeds and good company.

- Man can know one thing from its counterpart.

- It is useless to feel remorse on the actions which are out of one's control.

- Man's desire is based on the fact that its dark side is hidden from him

- Man's hatred is due to the fact that the dark aspect of the desire has come into light before him.

- When the love of a bad friend comes into your heart, the holy mosque of the heart will be destroyed and you too.

- Confession of ignorance which is real is better than price paid on remaining misguided.

- To get success by showing cleverness in the matters controlled by God is impossible.

- The inmates of Heaven will be simple in their ways.

- Intelligent persons utilize their intelligence in understanding the qualities and the virtues of God. The foolish spends his intelligence in understanding the worldly affairs.

- Knowledge and wealth in the possession of an unworthy person is like a sword in the hands of a robber.

- As a child does not know means to perform a work or make an excuse, he seeks the shelter of the mother, in every trouble.

- One who guides a blind man forty steps, his sins will be pardoned (Hadith).

- Answer to the questions of an uneducated and

unintelligent man is silence.

- Spirit of man is angelic, body is animal-like. He spends life in the confrontation of the two.

- If a man fulfils the needs of the spirit (soul) he is better than any angel. But if he is overpowered by physical desires, he is worse than an animal.

- Cleverness, greed and necrophagia are the qualities of a crow.

- Learning is for a short period of the human life, but the foolish considers it to be a lasting discovery of the secrets of the universe.

- One who does not leave the physical yearning is misguided.

- Progress which will occur by the love of God, will be His gift.

- Hell is the outcome of God's wrath

- Artificiality misguides. By removing it, the defects are brought to light.

- Artificiality attracts one towards himself and makes him selfish, but its removal discloses the temporary nature.

- Fall after worldly progress must be kept in mind by man.

- Belief in God by the whole world cannot increase the Might of God.

- I (God) was a hidden treasure, I wished that I may be known, so I brought in the Creation (Hadith). Emphasised by Maulana Rumi.

- Ego gives a false sense to man and let him believe

that he has a long life and there are chances for doing good in future, so let him enjoy the world for the time being.

- Grasping some points in understanding God, by a spiritual man is a gift of God.

- When man shows remorse over his sins, the blessings of God removes the broken heart condition.

- There is one artificial thing for every real thing. If one cannot distinguish between them, it leads to his destruction.

- If one is really blind, the blessings from God leads him.

- The cloud weeps with a heavy heart, but extends benefits to the earth.

- Enmity in the heart and praise on the lips does not please the praised one.

- God does not look into your beauty and wealth but takes into consideration your inner feelings and actions(Hadith). Emphasised by Maulana Rumi.

- When one is down with troubles and sadness, one does not show signs of happiness.

- Why will not the spiritual doctors be able to diagnose the spiritual ailments by observing signs. They even do not need to know the apparent signs.

- When a lover sacrifices himself, he gets an aroma of the beloved.

- When a person has been approved by God, his

actions cannot be wrong.

- One gains Heaven only from those actions which are unpleasant to his ego.

- The blessings of God are bestowed on a patient and broken heart

- Man is busy at first in the worldly affairs, but with the help of a spiritual person he can be better than angels.

- Without spirit the body is so lowly that it is buried under the earth.

- All the troubles that man encounters are punishments for his past actions, therefore he should not blame others.

- It is a bad quality in man, like that of Pharaoh, that he considers the real enemy, i.e. himself, faultless and picks enmity with others.

- The foolish is an enemy and the intelligent is our friend.

- The good intentioned actions of foolish man lead to troubles.

- The company of enemies converts a garden into a fireplace.

- A respectable age is according to knowledge gained and not by years.

- One should make himself lifeless in the hands of one, giving him the bath(spiritual).

- Mutual differences are due to ego.

- Man is enveloped with the troubles, although the canal of soul is so close to him, that he can clean them out (by water from the canal).

- Disgust towards world, obliges a man to search for goodness.

- One should seek Unity in Multiplicity.

- Hope is a proof of His (God's) presence.

- An old man in the family is like a prophet among the followers.

- One who is observing a matter himself, to give him information about it is useless.

- It is the demand of love that the lover should be aware of the mental awareness of the beloved.

- Rise in the position of the High ups, keeps them simple.

- He is wise who achieves the inner light.

- Knowledge is like a lamp and the real spiritual love is like the sun.

- On rising of the sun, the lamp becomes useless. In the same way, knowledge is helpless before real love.

- On complete sacrifice of the ego, nothing remains of the self, so there is no likelihood of his own loss.

- Emotions are hidden in the heart, drunkenness brings them out.

- If foolishness is personified, the darkness of the night will be put to shame.

- The one who has not got inner light will hanker after reason and will search for the path of signs.

- If knowledge is personified, the sun will appear dim before it.

- Remorse at odd times is not beneficial.

- It is only God's Grace that can purify the spirit (soul). Man's capability is only that he may clean himself from the apparent dirt.

- Complete wisdom is that precaution is taken before the occurrence of any trouble. Half wisdom is that one plans to get out of trouble at the time of trouble-eleventh hour.

- God can cure an incurahle ailment

- One should not be mild at inappropriate times, that the wife and the relatives may be spoiled.

- For every Pharaoh, a Moses is born.

- Man certainly gets the return of the virtues and the vices.

- If a man understands the signs from God in this world, he does not need clearing comments on the Day of Judgement.

- If a man cleans his heart, the life-after-death will be clear to him.

- Praise-worthy qualities are shadows of the heaven and the bad qualities shadows of hell.

- One should tell such things to people about religion which are appropriate to their understanding. Otherwise they will deny them.

- Affrunt to God and foolhardiness arc necessary for the administration of the Universe.

- One who devotes himself to God, God accepts him as His own.

- One who loves Me (God), I will kill him. Whom

I kill that way, I give him the reward i.e. Myself-quoted by Maulana.

- The drop of water which is mixed in a river is apparently lost, but in reality it has become safe.

- To sacrifice oneself for the sake of God is like getting the sea in exchange for a drop of water.

- For a drop of water to get mixed in river is an honor to the drop.

- As Satan has destroyed himself, he cannot tolerate to observe the virtues of any person, nor light from the lamp of virtues.

- Ego is drowned in a drunken condition that it is unmindful of the right path.

- You consider this world friendly? The Wealth whose beginning is from trouble, in the end it kicks a person and goes away.

- If a man cannot leave the worldly entanglements himself, they leave him themselves.

- How can the created know about the One who has created him. How can a particle know about creation of the Sun.

- Man struggles and the Grace of God bestows on him the ability.

- Fate is not in contradiction to capability. Capability remains along with the fate.

- A virtuous man gets nearness to God by repentance and crying.

- If a mother hits her child, the child then too seeks her shelter and hugs her.

- One who is in unison with God, goes round Him only. For him pain and pleasures are alike.

- One should acknowledge that this world is a field for the life-after-death. Whatever he will sow here will reap there.

- Looks are pleasant only when a purpose is hidden in them.

- Sleep is a sister of death.

- That the Dream is the result of observation in consciousness is wronz.

- The sign of creation of inner light in heart is that, one becomes disgusted with the world and is eager for the life-after-death (finality).

- Extreme happiness can become cause of death.

- Beggar bows for one Dinar, but the contented, kicks treasures.

- Worldly life and one after death are like two wives. If one is satisfied the other gets angry.

- So long as you are in a state of denial of Oneness of God, you will be void of the stage of Certainty.

- Man is not wise in reality from the worldly knowledge.

- To fulfill the desire of your Ego is idol worship.

- The intensity of wisdom is in crying for the love of God. One reaches the stage of sacrifice after that.

- At the time of death Sheikh Bu Ali Sena, when the life-after-death started revealing itself, acknowledged that in such matters the surmises based on acquired knowledge were useless.

- I am the boat in the river of souls. You can cross it through me (Hadith).

- Knowledge is like a rope.

- If a man studies the Holy Quran on the understanding that it was the word of God and spiritual in nature, his ego will be finished and he will get the path of reason.

- When you will finish your Ego and personality, then you will get the condition of living with God (so to say).

- The object of God by the Creation was to bring to light the hidden secrets.

- The real root of every reason is God.

- Physical diet is antagonist to spiritual diet

- Man eats food, but he is himself food for Hell. His example is like that of a goat who grazes, but the butcher is happy that it is grazing for his benefit.

- Every worldly ecstasy shuts man's ears and eyes

- One gets drunk with pride.

- Life is a dream and a dream makes a man forgetful of the reality.

- One should carefully observe the creation of God and should get himself lost in His greatness.

- When you concentrate on the creation by God, your own reality will be opened to you and you will keep quiet.

- Fire of Hell is a particle of curse and anger of God.

- Adopt state of humbleness and appreciate it. God will help you.

- The face of Reality appears bad to an atheist, but when man adopts humbleness the same face appears beautiful to him.

- Man's physical senses are weak but the inner soul is strong and a grand creation.

- If you put water in hot oil it will boil down the container and the stove will be spoiled.

- There is no need of oral teaching and advice when it reaches a man spiritually.

- If you cannot get the whole, do not leave it totally.

- Belief is a stage ahead of suspicion and surmise.

- As is the Ruler, so is the Ruled.

- God's mercy does not pay attention without the lamentations of the seeker.

- Men considers others according to his own capability. As he is, so he considers others likewise.

- A troubled man when he considers the troubles, are for his betterment, he does not remain sad and defeated.

- The existence of the Universe, is on love, and attraction.

- Men of strength safeguard their inner self, than care for the pearls and rubies.

- Roots are hidden under earth, but the signs appear in the leaves outside.

- A foolish man considers gold more valuable than life, but a wiseman considers giving away of wealth as charity for saving the life.

- If Adam did not have belief in the kindness of God, Satan would have been able to harm him.

- When troubles reach their climax, Mercy of God pays attention.

- Pain of waiting is sometimes more than the Pain of death.

- To search for a dry lump of earth in a canal, is equivalent to search for a fish on dry land.

- The height of liking is the extreme love.

- God loves those who love Him. Love is a quality of God.

- Prayers of a person close to God is for the love of God, and of a puritan is due to the fear of God.

- When a man performs good deeds, further paths of good deeds are opened for him. When he performs bad deeds, further paths of the bad deeds are opened for him.

- One who comes to know the secrets of God, keeps quiet as if his mouth is locked

- After once in trouble, only the fool gets ready to be entangled in the same trouble for the second time.

- Man should be thankful to God and think that God has not kept him in a worse condition.

- To complain on the distribution of graces by God, is a Denial of God.

- To put complaints about a friend before one's enemy is foolishness.

- With every good gift of God there is some irksome problem.

- Patience and forebearance is considered a treasure which does not come handy to every person

- If a man loves food, food too loves him.

- If a man observes patience he approaches near his goal.

- A woman's wisdom will be over-powered by man's, necessarily. Women too get impressed by man's external appearance.

- With spiritual nourishment man becomes holy like the Quran.

- The like of an imposter is like the sword of a eunuch.

- Hurry is Satanic, Composure (steadfastness) is bestowed by God.

- Heart is more reliable than face in beauty and virtues.

- A young man becomes old by constant troubles.

- However a man may be wise, the company of bad friends blinds him.

- All followers will be divided into 72 sects, only one will get deliverance - Hadith emphasized by Maulana Rum.

- When the God wants to keep someone lowly, then God's lover himself will not like to be high and honorable.

- The candle is devoured by Fire, but gives light to others.

- A lover will be wrong to think of rewards from the beloved for his services.

- A worshipper wishes rewards for his worships, but the lover of God wishes only to see the beloved.

- Lover's truth affects the unconnected person too.

- On account of the Truth of the Prophet PBH, the moon was split and the sun retraced itself.

- Man's body is made of earth. Great efforts are required to clean it

- Man likes to commit suicide on account of the difficulties and foolishness.

- When God wants to keep some one hungry there are many secret objects in it. The pain of hunger is better than the pain of disease.

- I (God) did not keep any differentiation among the prophets (Holy Quran)-emphasised by

Maulana.

- Do not concentrate on patience, but on the Patience-giver.

- The one who realizes the sea of Reality, his mind becomes open, so much so that he considers every occurance as the Will of God.

- The companion of the weak is often lowly.

- The existence of Satan is not contrary to the power of Man.

- Angels and Satan both influence our actions, but the power of control is in our hand.

- Satan is like God's dog. He gives trouble to the person who does not follow the path shown by God.

- The capability of control in man, is a gift from God.

- The control and power of God, does not destroy the power and control of a man in ordinary matters.

- You do not wish, but that which God wishes.

- God will forgive the sinners, but they will not get rewards which will be bestowed on the good souls.

- To give a speech in public for sake of praise is like making designs on a lump of earth which will not last.

- Take a lesson from the period of troubles.

- One who comes to know God, his tongue gets tied (He keeps silent).

- Fire of love never gets extinguished.

- The same thing is good for one but harmful for the other. (One man's food is a poison for the other).

- Real life is not of the body but of the soul.

- Concentrate on the gifts of God, not on His personality.

- Religion is the good advice.

- No doubt the day of separation is fixed.

- Oil and water are enemies of each other

- If you cannot control your ego, on eating the Barley bread, then take bread of the bran.

- Failure in the world is better in one way for man. A man whose all wishes have been fulfilled becomes rebellious and bad tempered.

- If you show mercy on the people on earth, God will have mercy on you.

- World is like a dead body liked by a dog.

- Worry about the sad moments is the forerunner of the pleasant moments.

- It is possible that in the worry your betterment is hidden.

- Something only heard cannot be equal (in certainty) to the one seen actually.

- Man should not be contended with an idea of God. He will not know God truly. Only when the imagination comes equal to the degree of vision, then it will be beneficial.

- Those who are free from intense desire of stomach and sex, only they will get the inner light.

- One thing is imaginary for one, but a reality for the other.

- He (God) only makes a man laugh and cry.

- Every secret ultimately comes out, so do not sow the seeds of bitterness because they will grow.

- There is no resemblance between sin and its result. As there is no resemblance between seed and its fruits.

- The troubles that a man gets mostly is the result of his past actions.

- Whoever practices Evil, he is responsible for it. Without doubt, God is in know of it.

- The imitator usually does not attain the stage of the reality. With small doubts, arising in the mind he will loose the balance.

- A puritan worries about as to what will be the ultimate result. A Godly person is perfect. He has the knowledge of the beginning and the end result. His fears are finished.

- Concentrate on the Maker and leave concentration on His creation.

- The beauties of the Nature are sometimes an obstruction in the right path

- One who disobeys God, does it at times with the idea of final support from Him.

- The worst punishment for a lover is the separation and indifference from his beloved.

- The creation by God is for the purpose that the Created may be benefitted from Him and not God Himself.

- All things move toward the Originality.

- A soft lump of earth is afraid of the rain, but a piece of stone is not afraid of it.

- Those who sacrifice their lives are in reality alive by the nectar of the Love of God. External life giving nectar is nothing for them.

- Die (sacrifice) before you die physically.

- Thorn is not liked by others, but is liked by fire, as it is its nourishment.

- Nature has deputed everyone for some work, according to his capability.

- The object of God is to test Man.

- Everything is busy in its work according to Nature.

- The origin of Creation is based on different elements and therefore they are at loggerheads.

- All the works of the world are dependent on hope.

- Man is very weak in keeping promises. He again reverts to those acts from which he sought pardon earlier.

- If a man has not seen the Reality, his attachment to a cause is worth pardon.

- There is no colour of the soul.

- Soul is recognized by soul. As such try to discover Aulia through your soul.

- Do not search for water, create thirst, water will come to you automatically. Do not worry about the object, but create an urge for it. The object will come to you automatically.

- The noble makes himself apparently ignorant of the criminal activities of others but he knows everything about them.

- In time of need rudeness is pardonable.

- One gets spiritual food in the company of Aulia Allah and he comes to know the inner secrets.

- The return of a part (soul) to Eternity should not cause grief.

- What is the higher spiritual attainment is to feel pleasure at the time of grief in heart.

- Sometimes one trouble of a man becomes a cause for relief from many troubles.

- A guiding lesson is not learned from book or speeches, but it is a gift of God. So pray to God.

- Man is unable to commit many sins during hunger, therefore he should be proud of it.

- Control, or lack of it, makes a man fit for reward or punishment.

- When God will take into account, Man's deeds, he will take into account only those over which he had control.

- Man should value the period when he has control over his actions.

- Persons of good deeds are a source of comfort for others. The Kafirs are a source of trouble to them.

- To help without personal object is a virtue of God. The same is the virtue of Aulia Allah (spiritual men).

- If anybody salutes the other (many a times)he does it with the object of a personal gain.

- Everything is destined to be destroyed, except God who will remain forever.

- It is usual with God that He does not postpone death or changes the fate.

- When the body is liquidated with Jehad and worship, the Soul becomes strong.

- One should have the strength of keeping God's secrets and not to move his lips.

- Loss of wealth and health becomes a cause for benefit of the soul and deliverance from the troubles. So it is the duty of man that he be a Mujahid and keep back the body and develop soul.

- All those body troubles which are by the Will of God act as worship and Mujahida, as if God engaged the person as a Mujahid by His order. Therefore the troubles become cause for being grateful to God.

- The reality of Heaven is beyond human comprehension.

- As man was lazy in worship, therefore God has fated troubles for him so that they may be a substitute of the worship.

- Occasionally troubles come for the benefit of a man.

- Life in this world is petty against the life after death

- One who is afraid of Death is actually afraid of himself.

- If a man gets any trouble, at times it is the result of causing torture to someone by his own action.

- In Heaven birds represent praise of God, tree - good deeds, canal of water - patience, canal of milk - emotion of love, canal of honey - love of worship and canal of wine - love of God.

- Anger is the seed of Hell.

- Light of religion extinguishes the fire of anger.

- Water extinguishes fire because fire burns all the

things which grow with the help of water.

- The world is wide for the worldly people but is narrow for the spiritual ones.

- Man should kick the apparent causes and consider the Real as the only One who created causes.

- Do not look down upon the black color.

- Philosophers consider God as the first Cause.

- One should be highly respectful and obedient to the Sheikh.

- It is the custom of the world that if you do not show friendliness towards your friends they become your enemy.

- In the company of the Beloved, a troublesome place too becomes a cause for pleasure. Hell is like heaven in the company of the Beloved.

- Heaven is hell in the continued absence of the Beloved

- Though you are human being apparently, but you have no human character in you.

- When death comes it does not give an opportunity to run away from it. The environment becomes tight.

- Do not consider death as death, it is entering in another life.

- If one comes into contact with the flame, he feels irritation and pain, but if he contacts spiritual light (Nur) the body feels pleasure.

- Love of God is a challenge. Sacrificial effort is its witness.

- Ego and Satan are the names of the same power, so are the Angels and Knowledge.

- In loaning, one should exhibit Charity and kindness, keeping in mind the benefits of after-life.

- The three stages of Reality are based on the Belief on surmise, belief on knowledge, and belief on seeing actually.

- If a Nabi is angry with his followers, it is due to his love for them.

- God gives good news at times. On sad occasions, do not grudge. May be you have many hidden benefits in it.

- God says if you are My Lover, you must be contented with My wishes. The lowly gets a high place after destruction (Fana) - emphasized by Maulana Rum.

- If a man gets tired on a journey he gets greater pleasure in rest.

- If one gets an object without effort, one does not value it.

- Troubles are steps towards completion of an object.

- The belief of personal relations with God, misguides.

- To come over the grief of separation, there is need for Qawwali.

- The spiritual dialogue cannot be heard from the physical ear.

- The signs towards death are a cause for happiness of the spiritual person.

- The example of union (Ittisal) is that two lamps are kept separate but their light is one.

- The love in the heart of a lover is the effect of the love in the heart of his beloved

- The attraction between male and female is due to the fact that one cannot complete work without the other.

- Disappointment in attaining the objects is a guide to Heaven.

- To go to Heaven one has to go through stages which are unpleasant.

- Many feel depressed in failure, but Muslims rise.

- If a crystal of Musk or Amber is broken the aroma will spread more.

- Spiritual men enjoy in poverty and hunger as a king enjoys Spring in Autumn.

- The prayer of the follower is based on a personal purpose but of the spiritual man on the love of God.

- The attraction of the beloved is such that the Lover does not feel it.

- The attraction of the beloved is hidden, but of the Lover is open.

- The sight of the beloved is like a life-giving nectar, one cannot die after it.

- God is the real friend and in the world the friend is one who is Godly in nature.

- The lover recovers senses on .getting aroma of the beloved

- Watch the whole universe, it came into being by a miracle.

- The lover is full of madness.

- The religions of Love and of the world are different.

- To hide the secret of love is like hiding a spark of fire in cotton.

- Blood is not washed by blood.

- The qualities of the extract of grapes (wine) are dependent on the looks of the Saqi.

- Apparently eloquent like a Tuti (a chirping bird), but the inner is silent and the soul is happy and fresh, are the qualities of a spiritual man.

- God fulfills desires (occasionally) without apparent cause.

- Fighting or showing temper is bad luck.

- Man should not consider anything petty or mean. It can be of use at any time in the future.

- Insight is far better than sight only.

- Laugh a little - lament a lot.

- To reach his heights, man requires a stress on his wisdom and tears in his eyes.

- God questioned in the beginning of Creation (Azal), "am I not your God". The reply was "certainly! why not". Now to prove our affirmation we are sent in this world to be tested by our actions, what we affirmed before God. - emphasized by Maulana Rum.

- If somebody does charity and prays, it is a proof

that the man has the virtue of Piety.

- Cat appears as if it is fasting but her face is only to get prey.

- Many a times praying in the beginning is to deceive others, then it becomes a habit, then God makes it a real worship for a man.

- Spiritual people too clean your heart.

- If a Sheikh gets Godly enlightment, it becomes apparent from his face. There is no need for the Sheikh to disclose it by his action.

- Patience in the time of trouble gives Solace.

- The belief in the reality is a strange blessing and nourishment. If somebody gets that, then there is no need for the physical diet.

- God fills the stomach, the bread is just a means.

- The river of inner pleasure is so vast that the seven seas are just like a drop in the ocean.

- Human cleverness and planning is not contrary to God's Mercy

- God shows mercy on the down trodden.

- The effect of a vicious eye is apparently dependent on the eye, but in reality its cause is the fate (destined by God).

- "SHIRK" (to believe in sharing of power of God by others) is an unpardonable sin.

- By adopting humbleness one get relieved of the lust for power.

- You sacrifice yourself for God. He will bestow eternal life to you.

- Vicious thoughts are like poisonous nails, they disfigure the face of the soul.

- The fulfillment of worldly desires is like making efforts which are unrewarding, like opening a tightly closed, but empty purse which has nothing in it.

- If there is no libido in man, then the obedience of the order of God against adultery carrles no meamng.

- The Prophet was shadowless like the flame of a lamp.

- When fire does not get the fuel, how peaceful it is, but flares up on getting the fuel.

- Only God will remain. Every body will come to believe that in the end existence of other things was temporary.

- When the lover totally gives up himself to the will of the Beloved, then only his physical body remains.

- Every thing in this world is like a morsel for the other which is developing itself like a morsel for another.

- To sacrifice your life for the pleasure of others is foolishness.

- Do not become like sugar, for the lust of the worldly people, but become poison to them.

- Excepting God a thing destroys the other and in turn is itself destroyed by another one.

- The Sheikh of the period gets reflection of the Prophet PBH.

- The man doing cruelty to weak must know that there is something more powerful than himself.

- God punishes without His apparent arms and hands.

- Good life is that by which one develops closeness to God.

- The more one gets resources to meet the beloved, the desire dwindles down, in him.

- To adhere intensely to the worldly life is not wisdom ·

- Man should try for a fresh development. Every time he gets a stage higher of the development, he is in a fresh existence.

- Bad circumstances after good are very painful.

- It is a curse on man that his soul has been kept in the body which is of different origin.

- The old garments appear new on a noble person (H) - Hadith emphasized by Maulana Rum.

- Islam appears strange to the unfit.

- For one who gets inner light from God, the old age is not harmful.

- Beauty is in fact a possession of God. All virtues belong to God and the Universe is a window for them.

- If a man curtails his necessities and spends money on the needy, he will get reward for it in after-life.

- World is in fact non-existent, but appears to be existing. Life after death is in fact existing but appears non-existing.

- The knowledge of light of God comes in the heart spiritually only, and not by the oral or book teaching.

- If a man is busy through out in, worldly matters, he will be ignorant of life-after-death.

- Man should water fruit-bearing trees and not the bushes of thorns.

- To apply "Surma" in ears is foolishness.

- As much as a man controls his ego and desires he is destined to rise.

- Faithfulness is the essence of the qualities of a man.

- A man with a cut-nose wants to see every body in that condition.

- Knowledge is the real nucleus, words are like kernels. Less the kernel the bigger is the nucleus.

- Women have more patronizing qualities, but they suffer from jealousy, such as when a man has two wives.

- The soul of a spiritual man is like moon light, which if it falls on a dirty thing, it itself remains pure.

- Prayer without intention and concentration of the heart and mind is not the real prayer.

- There is a difference in crying during the prayer, one type of cry is the soul of prayer, the other spoils the prayer.

- Greed of a man makes him see a vice as a virtue.

- Libido is most dangerous for man.

- If the worldly friends go against you in this world, you should thank God that you have come out of their entanglement and will get opportunity to search new friend.

- The unfaithfulness of worldly friends is sometimes a blessing in disguise from God. for you.

- When God is merciful to someone, He creates such situations that the man breaks his worldly attachments.

- Man should adopt means for his achievements but should not ignore the "Final Cause" responsible for the apparent causes.

- God values tears. Do not consider shedding of the tears is unnoticed by God.

- Shedding one tear out of fear of God is equal to one drop of blood of a martyr. And sighing and crying before God is a recommendation for man.

- Religious people believe that God has control on all happenings. He can do away the oncoming trouble on sighing and crying. The philosopher thinks that all are natural happenings beyond the control of God, therefore sighing and crying is useless.

- Crying before God creates happiness in the heart of a man

- God makes troubles as means for final and higher attainments so you should be patient on His orders. Love is hidden in the cruelty somtimes.

- His (God's) order makes every impossible as possible.

- All godly people keep an eye on the First Cause in every matter.

- Drugs have their effect but if the drug does not act, they consider it to be a wish of God.

- Death of a Momin is such as the disintegration of a prison house for a prisoner.

- This body will not be there in heaven but the soul will be alive, God will keep it alive and bestow spiritual nourishment and diet.

- More a man keeps himself away from the worldly diet the more he will be fit for spiritual nourishment.

- When a man leaves physical nourishment and waits for spiritual nourishment, he will get it.

- The sunlight first falls on the top of mountains (metaphorical).

- God will change the vices of the noble people into virtues.

- Man's ideas and desires will take shape on the day of judgement.

- A Worldly man likes, greatly the pride, the wealth and power, because of self aggrandizement.

- If one swears by Love, after that every act is a negation (KUFR) except the servitude of the Beloved.

- Tearing of clothes gives solace to a maniac.

- A maniac loses control over rhythm.

- A man trying to understand by observation will understand according to the capability of the vision in his eyes.

- There is no beginning or end in the matter of love.

- Just a sign is sufficient for understanding by a wise man.

- The character of father is sufficient for understanding the character of the son.

- The one who observes patience in the worldly matters is worthy of respect.

- Sacrifice yourself for God then only you will get the eternal life.

- Crooked legs cast crooked shadows.

- The Eternity is not based on differing elements (as in the world), so there is eternal life in

- If something cannot be acquired completely, it should not be left out totally.

- The company of the bad people is very strong in creating sickness of the soul.

- Wherever you graft, it is the part of the original tree.

- If wine is kept in any container it will remain wine.

- In the condition of uncertainty, man becomes oppressed.

- The joy and ecstacy produced by the prayers is lasting and that produced by the sin is temporary.

- Every action performed in this world is under God's control.

- Man is atheist by argument of his knowledge, but

does not realize the low limits of the knowledge that he possesses.

- After adopting piety, a man's heart directs him towards virtues automatically.

- There is no state of hesitation in the state of Patience.

- Adam acknowledged his mistake but Satan held God responsible for it.

- Man should not make God's wish as always in response to his own mistakes.

- Thinking of the fate only makes a man misdirect his conscience towards the evil and makes his body lazy.

- The particles of the body brighten up in the light of the Sun apparently, but the spiritual thoughts are brightened by the knowledge of God.

- Poverty is so dangerous, that at times they adopt Kufr.

- Man looses everything in the pursuit of the world. Then he feels shy to move towards the "Ultimate".

- He is the best man who benefits others.

- To live along with ordinary persons (public) is Prophet's tradition.

- The worship of perishable gods is bad.

- If one has righteous heart there is no dearth of friends. Make friends with others and see the ever growing numbers of friends around you.

- A friend is necessary in the path of life.

- A Travel companion should be chosen after test. He should be a Good person.

- He is the friend whose wisdom is your support.

- Pleasure is living in the (good) company.

- Repentance and crying is beneficial before death to seek pardon of the punishment after death.

- When ego of man presses him towards sin, he should think of God.

- In old age too, repentance is better than indifference towards past sins.

- Lonely traveller does not remain satisfied. Co-travellers travel in comfort.

- Do not repent on what damage you have done by accident.

- Different thoughts enter the brain (heart) of a man. Sometimes they are directed towards evil, at other times he hates them.

- God has created me by His Grace without my right.

- Though I am unfit, but if He shows Mercy to me, nothing will effect God, adversely.

- Worldly people are like children who waste their time in play.

- A thirsty man is awakened simply by hearing the sound of running water.

- Love and sleep are antagonist.

- Lamp is bright on burning only.

- Wine and singing are similar in the quality, that

carries one up to the other.

- Singing is the beginning of love, wine is the upper limit.

- Extreme closeness sometimes creates suspicion.

- Extreme silence gives away the secret.

- Man's desire increases more when he is prohibited from doing something.

- Sacrifice your ego. So long as you have physical qualities and desires, you will not get spiritual secrets.

- Only after crossing the stages of observation & sacrifice, you will have the knowledge of God.

- The Negative of anything becomes the proof of its existence, sometimes.

- The denial of existence of other gods can be a step to know the true God.

- Death is not the reason to take one to the grave but it is change in the quality of the body.

- Think that all persons are in the agony of death. This will create in man's heart repentance and mercy and destroy the idea of enmity towards others.

- This world is like a prison for a Momin.

- The one who is fully aware of life-after-death, his face appears enlightened in a peculiar way.

- An evil man sees evil in the virtue as well.

- When one becomes one with i.e. identifies himself completely, with God, he starts saying like Mansur that I am God.

- You will get knowledge of God when you give up the knowledge of other than God i.e. fake gods.

- Money is necessary for the work in this world, but the love of God is necessary for life after-death, so is the repentance.

- If a person wants a customer, who will be a better customer than God.

- If you cry in love of God you will get Hauz-e-Kauser in place of the few drops of your tears.

- Wise man loves the "Reality" as it is lasting forever.

- If a man is truthful to his religion then he can understand the truth in the heart of a man of other religion. He will not be cruel to him.

- When you allow cruelty in any true religion then you are not perfect in your religion.

- The beginning of a false promise is pleasant but the end is frustration.

- The eyes which differentiate only colors cannot differentiate souls.

- When one branch is cut, its nourishment and strength appears in the other branch.

- If a man fixes belief on one aspect so much that he cannot think of other possibility, then God allows him an action to take place according to his belief, such as walking on water.

- To remain Steady is the quality of God.

- God's one day is equal to one thousand years (Holy Quran). - emphasized by Maulana Rum.

- The progress achieved on others support is not lasting.

- God accepts even the fake because His object is not profit

- A branch tied to another tree will not work as well as the original tree.

- Zulekha became young under the influence of Hazrat Yusuf (PBH).

- The Dates tree, which was dry and fruitless, became full of fruits under the influence of Holy Mary.

- Man should not give up self correction on getting hopeless by his previous evil deeds.

- Every hidden matter is recognized by its external signs, like water from the grass outside.

- Man loves worldly things on the basis of external signs. Then why should he not love the Originator of those signs.

- If a man wants to free himself, he should overlook the beginning and concentrate on the end result.

- Man is not satisfied over what is present, but struggles for the non-existent.

- It is a blunder to consider the signs of destruction as signs of relief.

- The Patience of moon in the dark nights, brightens it up. The patience by of a flower in company of thorns, creates aroma in it.

- By observing patience Prophets have reached their highest stages of achievement.

- You love for your present being. It is like love of an existant for a non-existant.

- Death is a bridge which carries a friend to his Friend (God).

- Froth itself is a lowly thing, its movement and life is dependent on the river.

- You should melt your body by extreme efforts to get God's attention.

- Teaching creates search, that only works for the achievement.

- Real poverty is physical. Man may melt his physical body, but should not beg for alms.

- Parts are proof of the existence of the Full (complete).

- When you leave your ego and sacrifice your personality (for God), then your actions will not remain yours (responsibility).

- To put something out of place is cruelty.

- Truth is bitter.

- Laugh a little but cry a lot. The ultimate result of crying is laughing.

- The company of a Pir is better than reading and meditation.

- If a man starts talking about a good thing, the lengthening of the discourse may bring him to evil result.

- Innocents and Prophets do not speak lies.

- The Prophet PBH use to ask his companions to include him in their prayers.

- To give a lecture according to the intelligence and capability of listeners, is wisdom.

- When there are no troubles there is no patience and when there are no short-comings there is no humbleness.

- When God will call you His own, all your pains and troubles will disappear.

- In any case the beloved is not ignorant of the lover.

- The life in the Universe is dependent on different conditions and hopes.

- Jihad minor is the Jihad with the non-believers, Jihad major is the Jihad with your own Ego.

- Effectiveness is given by God, other sources are ineffective.

- Man would feel hopeless if his efforts for an action are based on the knowledge only, but there is no hopelessness if the efforts are based on love for the beloved.

- God created man without the object of personal gain. So man should give up himself to God without selfishness.

- The acceptance of prayer by God is based on the capability of correct and earnest praying.

- If one gives up himself totally, to God, he looses his own ego. God accepts him as His own.

- God is one, but His oneness is not of count, but that there is no partner to Him.

- When the ego and personality leaves the mind of

the servant of God then he does not exist spiritually, thereafter only God remains.

- The burden of God's decisions is carried patiently by the love and selflessness of a lover of God.

- When you will bear patiently with the evils of evil-doers you will be the true follower of the habits of the Prophet PBH.

- The prayer is accepted of the one who is nearer to God.

- Man struggles for his self only but the running of the whole world administration and peoples' benefits are associated with it.

- The same thing which was a cause for salvation can become a cause for destruction

- Sadness can be a cause for happiness and happiness be a cause for sadness

- When surmise is based on some reality then definitely there is a Creator of that reality on whose account the surmise appeared.

- Truth is obliged to falsehood, as the truth has been adopted due to existence of the falsehood.

- God created counter parts together, like thorns and buds of flowers.

- Correct judgement is a great boom which discloses everything in reality

- Remove the curtain from the causes and see the first Cause (or cause of the causes).

- Tears are necessary for the earnest prayer.

- God bestow tears in my eyes so that my actions

mav be fruitful.

- Momin is simple and gentle.

- As mother does physical work for the young child, in the same way God will support the Momin.

- Every body wishes God to be on his side, though he may follow a wrong way for His approval.

- There are many inner signs of relation with God, but it is not proper to disclose them.

- If goodness is used out of place it can become a mischief and if mischief is practiced at the proper place it can become goodness.

- There is no chance of a deliberate or non-deliberate mistake on having proper consultations earlier.

- Learned people are successors of the Prophets. They got the knowledge in succession.

- Aloofness & seclusion are against man's interest as he is deprived of the benefits from the learned and enlightened persons.

- The place where Moses met Prophet Khizr, there was the eternal life-giving stream. Therefore the fish got alive and escaped into sea. - emphasized by Maulana Rum.

- Tongue is nourished by the ideas in the heart(mind). What is in your heart comes out of the tongue.

- It is the duty of the disciple that he keeps his gaze fixed on his Sheikh. The company of the Sheikh is very beneficial.

- The lovers of God are continuously busy in talking to God through prayers.

- If a Lover is asked to see his beloved occasionally, it is equivalent to that he is being asked to see himself occasionally.

- There are the people whose sins will be changed into good deeds by God (Q.). emphasized by Maulana Rum.

- Cash is better than keeping a debt.

- A greatest sinner, like me, requires greatest Mercy of God.

- The signs of goodness appear on the forehead as the green grass points to the fact that there is water in the subsoil.

- Any matter which is disagreeable to a man of clear conscience, it is certainly an advance signal of some oncoming trouble.

- People do not worship a setting sun.

- If a man takes spiritual nourishment by praying to God, then his spoken words will be effective.

- Those who use their wisdom are in peace.

- One must try to get company of the good people. If you want to see its effect see the oil that acquires aroma in company of flowers.

- The one who benefits others from his grave too, is not dead. Dead is the person who does not extend benefit to others.

- He is the real traveler whose eyes are fixed on the destination.

- Who will fulfil his promises more than God Himself.

- A king becomes a slave of a beautiful girl.

- The kingdom of knowledge is more comforting.

- To depend on the apparent good is a mistake.

- Man concentrates on "QIBLA" but forgets the entity who made Qibla (God).

- Jinn fill up their stomach with aroma, angel get their nourishment by worship.

- If fruits fall automatically from some recess, then if we call it a tree, it will not be wrong.

- One gets right outlook in the company of godly persons.

- From God one gets that benefit which is real and he reaches his object.

- Every Prophet had grazed goats.

- (Holy) Quran has kept secret of "Soul" (Spirit) by calling it to be the Order of God. It cannot be understood by any example.

- God cannot be addressed "Where" because His place is limitless.

- Man is not beyond God's control at any time.

- Man is sometimes empty of thoughts and sometimes full of thoughts. It proves that he is under control of a Creator.

- If a man requests something from the other man, it is like a beggar asking for alms from another beggar.

- To want help from the worldly people is as if to request another prisoner for his own release.

- One can request help from a godly person.

- Happiness is not dependent on the causes only. It depends on the peace of mind as well.

- To search happiness in wealth and palaces is foolishness.

- Our troubles are mostly self created.

- The view of the water gets concealed by foam. Similarly the treasures of spirit/soul get concealed by the decorations of the body.

- The miracles of Prophets are not dependent on material things.

- If a man concentrates on the result from the very beginning, he will be saved from the deceit.

- The attachment to God does away with the ego and desires.

- Every living being is in trouble due to physical desires.

- To find an excuse to do good, is good but to find excuse to do evil is evil.

- The dead are not allowed to speak, because they have come to know the secret of life. If they will speak then the hidden secrets will be out.

- The administration of the Universe is running but the ignorance of man persists.

- When a farmer reaps his farm, the result of the sowed seeds comes to li.ght. Life after death is its example.

- Milk taken out of the breast cannot be returned.

- Taking back a gift after giving it, is like a dog licking his vomit.

- To return a gift from friend is bad.

- The antagonists are sometimes hidden in one. like fire hidden in hot water

- Charity brings one closer to God and he gets affluence in his property.

- A man is more greedy of a prohibited thing.

- It is a quality of the Holy Quran that many people go stray by it, but whose hearts/mind are alert and well informed they obtain the right path.

- There is one sect (of Philosophers) which denies the Reality and thinks everything as imaginary (Softai).

- Godly person, whom God has selected to guide can be requested for full attainment of an object.

- Beauty can be compared with opium.

- Prophets have told that whatever you wish by ego, it will grow like thorns.

- A little attention by Sheikh is better than your own hundred plans.

- You cannot reach stage of self sacrifice without extreme love of God.

- Hope and fear point to the real belief.

- The sleep of a learned man is better than the worship by an illiterate.

- Attainment of higher position depends upon intention and good behavior.

- Even when you are not one with the beloved, it is better to be as close as possible.

- Stand by (God's) order. Stand by wish of God.

- An ordinary person has hundreds of desires in his heart. But there is only one desire in the heart of a lover, to get his beloved.

- To travel with some body, may be a blind person, is better than traveling alone.

- An arrow does not fly without a bow, so a disciple cannot rise without a Sheikh.

- When Love was born, Patience died.

- For the eye which is not destined to see the beloved. it is better for that eye to be blind.

- God is with you wherever you are.

- The cause of delay in the fulfillment of prayer (desire) of a Momin is, that God the Great wants to keep him engaged with Him.

- Truth is satisfaction. Lie is suspicion.

- Man's heart is satisfied when he hears a true story.

- Experts can differentiate between Truth and Falsehood when uttered before them.

- Sometimes God makes a man's going stray ar occasion to get belief in God, at other times a person observing prayers is lead astray.

- To pardon the sin of a sinner is the hidden mercy of God.

- If the disbeliever had not denied God, there was

no need of miracles to occur at times.

- Sometimes peace is hidden in fear and benefits are hidden in troubles.

- It is usual that instead of attaining loved objects, the lover gives up himself to them.

- Worldly thoughts are like dreams in the sleep.

- Often women are the basis of quarrel and fight.

- Life of a lover is spent as if in a box full of sorrows.

- Anything which we do not like for self, we should not like for others.

- God sometimes rewards a person for his deeds, even before the day of judgment.

- We all are smeared with sins committed by us.

- Give up your total personality to a godly man (spiritual man) so that no matter remains in it, which could be caught in by the flames of Hell.

- The condition of intense desires cannot be expressed in words.

- When soul gets free of physical pleasures, spiritual secrets start revealing before man.

- The good thoughts originating from bottom of heart are lasting.

- The Prophet PBH had given permission that when you do not get God's words, work with your own wisdom.

- Man should protect himself from the air of the pride, otherwise it will finish him.

- Whe'n a person attains the stage of believing "The Unseen", he, as if, attains permanent kingship.

- The challenge to God is done by a man with filled stomach. The hungry has not got Pharaoh's habit.

- Even the old age of the worldly persons do not release them of childhood.

- If one does not attain wisdom in old age, he is like a child.

- Show the right path to my people, as they are ignorant (Hadith). - emphasized by Maulana Rum.

- Acquisition of wealth beyond one's need is harmful.

- There is one more world above the physical one, which affects the latter.

- In mother's heart a strange flame burns for the love of her children.

- In reality the reason for going stray is the ego of man.

- Man can distinguish between the winds arising from the fireplace and the breeze of a garden.

- The difference between truth and falsehood is such as between the odor of musk and garlic.

- The difference between friendship and bitterness is such as between incense of (Benzoin) and Asafatida.

- Get in touch with the Great Spirit. The way to it is by leaving ego and sacrifice of personality.

- One who devotes himself to godly deeds, God Himself enlightens his world.

- He is the real Mujahid who struggles against his ego.

- If the world comes to you by itself then approve it.

- Man should pass over the stage of indecisiveness and worry, but should concentrate on the Personality (God) who created him.

- Slow and steady is successful in all his planning.

- Patience is half belief (Hadith). - emphasized by Maulana Rum.

- I am proud of my contentment.

- A Momin should respect his guest.

- Meditation for a short time is better than worship of a year without meditation.

- A Faqir is master of his time and Father of his time.

- Miser of the world is often benevolent. Those who do not waste money on themselves are very often philanthropist.

- You have to return to your God.

- Man's worry at times is a cause for peace and comfort.

HAZRAT BU ALI QALANDER

HAZRAT SHEIKH BU ALI QALANDER - His full name was Sheikh Abu Ali Sharf Uddin Bin Salar Fakhre Uddin. He was Sufi Saint of India. His ancestry goes up to Imam Abu Hanifa. His father came to India from Iraq in 600 H / 1201 A.D. and was a learned man. His father's first marriage was with the daughter of Hazrat Bahauddin Zakaria of Multan, After her death, he married the sister of Maulana Neamat Ullah Hamadani-Bibi Hafeeza. Hazrat Bu Ali was born out of that wed lock. He acquired sufficient knowledge at an early age. For about 20 years he gave teachings and discourses near Qutub Minar Delhi.. When he became a Sufi, he left the madarsa, threw away the books in river and went to Panipat in the condition of trance. He settled in Baghoti and Budha Khera of Panipat. H Bu Ali Qalander was attached to Hazrat Nizam Uddin Aulia. Sheikh Shamsuddin Turk stayed with Hazrat Bu Ali in Panipat at the instructions of Hazrat Nizam Uddin. Sheikh Jalal Uddin Mohammed of Panipat was benefitted spiritually in the company of Hazrat Bu Ali Qalander and became his Khalifa, later on. Hazrat Bu Ali died in Karnal and was buried there but it is said that his relatives quietly shifted his body at night to Panipat. He had two Mathnavi to his credit, depicting intense love of God.

SAYINGS OF HAZRAT BU ALI QALANDER

1.   The height of obligation is its completion.

2.   A Spiritual man is recognized by another spiritual man.

3.   To belong to the same species depends on inner
      qualities and not on physical resemblance.

4.   To be thankful to God increases the number of
      gifts from Him.

5.   One who observed patience, got respect, one
      who was greedy got dishonor.

6.   A person believing in God is free of hesitation.

7.   Those who are in real love, feel fresher than
      when out of it.

8.   Love is a disease, but it has the soul of health.
      Its troubles are a source of comfort.

9.   Respect Shariat.

10.   If earning bread would have been dependent on
      special prayers (Darud, etc.) then nobody would
      have been richer than Molvis.

11.   Wazaifs (special prayers) are not for seeking
      worldly gains.

12.   Kick away the throne of Khusro. Give away your
      head but do not beg in order that you may keep
      your honor.

13.   One says he is Sheikh (Sufi) and keeps the
      string of rosary beads in his hand, but Oh!, idol
      - worshipper, you keep hidden idols in your
      heart.

14.   Why are you standing for prayer, your heart/
      mind is in your cows and ass, Oh pretender.

15.   God! Save me from the love of the world, for
      bread and wealth. sacrifice your body for them.

16.   Your heart is never free from desires and

wishes. Never you concentrate by heart, in prayers.

17. Worldly people, for getting silver and gold, if it comes handy, sacrifice their bodies.

18. You want God too and world as well. The implementation of this thought is impossible and is madness.

19. Your ego is mischievous, which like a dog, catches the hand of a thief and pulls it down.

20. I know little of what is the reality of love. Love is nourished by the beauty of the beloved.

21. Those who sacrifice themselves in love, get new lives. In every period they are obliged by the unknown.

22. What is piety and prayer, Oh great man! It is to be unsuccessful in self's desire (ego).

23. Your life is like water in a canal. When it moves forward it never comes back.

24. Love and faithfulness have disappeared from this world, which means that the human character is finished.

25. Be thankful to God, so that God may bestow on you what you deserve.

26. The view of the beloved (God) is not hidden from you. But it is the defect of your vision.

27. It is discovered that to repent and pray do not carry weight, but the real acceptance depends on God's favor.

28. Anybody favored by God will get the strength in his heart.

29. Spiritual men declare openly "we do not love worldly things which are destined to destruction".

30. Man cannot observe vices in his beloved, nor can tolerate to listen about her vices.

31. How busy is the universe is a secret, known to God only.

HAZRAT NIZAM UDDIN AULIA

HAZRAT NIZAM UDDIN AULIA - From 636 H to 725 H. He is remembered as Mahbub-Ilahi, Sultan-ul-Mashaikh and Aulia. One more title of Shams-ul-Mulk was given by Sultan Ghias Uddin Balban, His real name was Mohammed and his ancestry goes up to Hazrat Ali. His family shifted from Bukhara to Lahore. Then his maternal grandfather Khwaja Arab shifted to Budaun with his family. Hazrat Nizam Uddin was born in Budaun. He became an orphan at the age of 5 years. He was brought up by his mother. He got early education from Maulana Ala Uddin. He shifted to Delhi, in search of acquiring further education. His mother accompanied him. He was then 16 years in age. Here he became a disciple of Maulana Shams Uddin, Maulana Kamal Uddin & Maulana Ahmad Tabrezi. Then he went to Pak Pattan to meet Baba Farid Ganj Shakar. At that time his age was 20 years. Baba Sahab adopted him as his Khalifa on the very first day. He stayed with the Baba from 655 to 656 H. He became so famous for his spirituality that hundreds of people used to become his disciples daily. Sultan of Delhi also became his disciple. Sultan Qutub Uddin had enmity with him. Among his other disciples were Hazrat Amir Hasan Sanjri and Hazrat Ameer Khusro. His famous books are "Fawaid-ul-Fawad" and "Fasle Farad" besides 12 others. The former were compiled by Khwaja Hasan Sanjri.

Sayings of Hazrat Nizam Uddin compiled mainly from Fawaid-ul-Fawad:

(1)   He used to emphasize the need to be sympathetic to people in distress.

(2)   Do not hoard wealth

(3)   Feeding others is liked in all the religions.

(4)   God sometimes bestows Prophethood to a cattle grazer. Otherwise how can he deserve prophethood.

(5)   A thing worth of value in love is steadfastness.

(6)   One should be obedient to God and be very courteous to the public

(7)   Wherever you stay, be open hearted and truthful

(8)   When a person becomes learned, he gets Honor. When he is obedient to God, his actions are better. At that time a guardian (Pir) is needed so that he may not become proud of his learning and actions.

(9)   Devotional Music is a touch-stone for men, (they may go astray on hearing music).

(10) Some people are of the nature that the more they hoard wealth, the more greedy they become.

(11) The purpose of hoarding Gold and Silver should be, to benefit others.

(12) When anybody comes across an unpleasant situation, he should be patient and should not complain about it. He should think that it is the Will of God.

(13) If you do not get Prosperity, do not be sorry over it. But you must maintain your Love for God.

(14) If you listen to poetry, you get interested in it. If poetry is recited in a musical voice, it increases your interest. It is the Devotional Music which kindles fire of Love of God

(15) Those who perform Idol-worship and are Heathens throughout, the punishment from God that they will get, will be permanent likewise. Otherwise Momins do not commit sins throughout (as they do not perform idol-worship).

(16) In Sufism, one should start with a wish (Salam) first, when somebody comes to him. Then the Sufi should entertain him with food and then talk.

(17) I forgive the person who speaks ill of me.

(18) To wish ill of a person is worse than speaking ill of him.

(19) Hazrat Nizam Uddin emphasized the Ayat, that anybody who fears God, He creates means of Bread for His servant, from such sources that the person cannot imagine about them.

(20) God treats men with Justice and benevolence. But men practices besides justice and benevolence, Cruelty as well.

(21) The Sufi is one who is not happy with any (worldly) thing, nor sorry for its absence. He is the man who has relinquished the world.

(22) Those who serve food (to others) should themselves take food afterwards.

(23) Steadfastness and Punctuality are very effective, in performance of any undertaking.

(24) If anybody speaks ill of the other, the listener should be capable of differentiating Truth from Falsehood and know whether the person speaking ill, has g ot some vested interest in it or not.

(25) Learned people are full of Knowledge. Sufis are full of Love (of God) that overshadows knowledge. The Prophet have both Knowledge and Love (of God).

(26) As Libido at a wrong time and place is prohibited, so is the anger.

(27) If somebody tenders advice to somebody, he should not do it in public, but in private. The advice before public takes the shape of admonition.

(28) There are three types of Repentance (Toba). One for the Past, one for the Present and a third for the future (that he may not repeat that sin).

(29) To give freedom to a slave is like kindling life in a dead body.

(30) If somebody commits sin, his face is away from God and his back is towards God. When he repents and seeks His pardon, then his face is towards God.

(31) To give ten coins in charity to poor, is better than spending one coin on himself.

(32) Considering that you have defects in yourself and you do not point out the defects of others, you are a gentleman.

(33) The daily "Istekhara Prayer" (Namaz-e-Istekhara) is for the safety of that day.

(34) Haj takes you towards "Kaba" the "Pir" takes you towards God directly (so-to say).

(35) It is better that the person should be buried at the same place (town) where he has died.

(36) Hazrat Nizam Uddin emphasized the saying of Hazrat Syedna Imam Umar that "When you do not show your love to children, how can you expect patronage from elders."

(37) To remain absent is better than be present. but inattentive

(38) There are three types of persons - Those who are attached to the world, the others who are estranged towards world and the third type are those who are neither attached nor estranged towards world.

(39) Do not hoard wealth, but that which is necessary and distribute the rest. Hoarded Stones and Gold are on equal footing.

(40) Anything which is not given as charity for the sake of God is a wasteful expenditure. (besides that for basic necessities) If you distribute your whole wealth for the sake of God, you will not be spend-thrift.

(41) A Pious person is one who has not committed

any sin. The Repentant (Taib) is one who committed sin, but is repentant and has sought God's pardon. The Taib has stronger Will that he does not revert to the pleasure of the sin, which he enjoyed earlier.

(42) Nobody can stop, what God Wills to give (to His servant).

(43) Hazrat Nizam Uddin emphasized the saying of Hazrat Aisha PBH that "He is a bad man who starts thinking himself as Good."

(44) One who really loves Knowledge and learned people, is pardoned for his sins

(45) Real Love is following in the footsteps of the Beloved.

(46) If somebody is sad and in a difficult situation, he should ponder as to why is he in that position. The adamant attitude does not take him out of that difficult situation.

(47) If one is sarcastic towards anybody for his drawback he should first think whether he suffers from the same drawback or not.

(48) Even if he has no drawback he should be thankful to God and not be sarcastic towards others.

(49) Hazrat Nizam Uddin RAA emphasized the saying of Hazrat Sh. Saif Uddin that "If somebody is ill-treating me (even then) I shall do good to him."

(50) Jealousy is bad but not the competitive spirit (Rashk).

(51) In all the works in which Ego and vested

interest are involved, there is no Grace of God and benevolence on them. The person may follow a crooked path and end up in failure.

(52) For every undertakin.g, good intentions are necessary.

(53) Inherent quality is not ever lost, but the acquired one is temporary and not ever lasting.

(54) Capability of man to do aood is dependent on his power and obedience to God.

(55) Good actions (Amal) cannot be performed without (Ilm) knowledge to do it. Knowledge (Ilm) and Practice (Amal) are both interconnected.

(56) One should believe that his actions are always in the knowledge of God.

(57) God has always kept hidden a group of His friends (Aulia).

(58) Knowledge gifted from God is "Shariat".

(59) To make excuses in Love is contrary to true love. It is the behavior of a stranger and not of a lover.

(60) He is a highly mean person, who poses himself as a Spiritual man and actually he is not. He is a very good man who is spiritual but does not show off.

(61) Openness is antagonistic of Malice (Kudurat).

(62) An imposter Sufi is a mean and a degraded person. Whatever he does, he does it to satisfy his Ego.

(63) Friendship is exhibited in being in agreement with a person. Antagonism (generally) shows

enmity with him.

(64) A wealthy man depends on his wealth, but a poor man depends upon God.

(65) The real value of Contentment in poverty is after abandoning wealth, not when he continues to think of wealth and ponders over his poverty.

HAZRAT BURHAN UDDIN GHARIB

HAZRAT BURHAN UDDIN GHARIB from 654 H / 1256 A. D. to 738 H / 1337 A. D. He was an Indian Sufi, who was also called Qutub Alamdar and Bayazid the Second. He belonged to a family, high up in spirituality, living in Hansi, where he was born. He got his early education from his learned uncle. He did not marry. He traveled to Delhi and got spiritual benefit from Khwaja Nizam Uddin-Mahbub Ilahi. He made Sh. Burhan Uddin supervisor of the kitchen of his Khanqah. He was given "KULHA", by Mahbub Ilahi, after he had completed his training. Sh. Sahab greatly loved his teacher, who asked him to go to Deccan. Sh. Sahab took the plea that he would be away, that way from the shoes (Nalain) of his Pir, which too he greatly respected. Hazrat Mahbub Ilahi asked him to take away the Nalain of his Pir, along with him. Then Sheikh Sahab said that he would be away from the meetings (Majlis) of his Pir. Actually he was diffident to leave his Pir. Hazrat Mahbub Ilahi asked him to take along with him all the disciples who were present then. Their number was nearly one hundred, at that time of the meeting. He complied with the order of his Pir, took along with him all the disciples present then, who too willingly compiled their Pir's wishes. They all came to Daulatbad and spread Islam in Deccan and also corrected the ethical status of the Muslims over there. He died in Khuldabad and was buried there. He was very interested in "SAMA" Nasir Uddin Faruqi named a new town after his name, i.e. Burhanpur.

Addressing his disciples he said: (1) This world is like a shadow. When a person directs his face towards it, it goes ahead and when a person turns his back towards it, it follows him; (2) He advised his disciples to struggle for the good of others. He gave an example that a tree stands in the sun but gives shade-cover to others. wood burns itself, but gives comfort to others; (3) When a person reaches his zenith of spiritual development, he starts seeing clearly his own faults.

HAZRAT MAKHDOOM JEHANIAN JEHAN GASHT

HAZRAT MAKHDOOM JEHANIAN JEHAN GASHT - From 707 H / 1303 A. D. to 785 H 1384 A. D. He was son of Syed Ahmad Kabir. His grandfather Syed Jalal Uddin Surkh migrated to Multan from Bukhara. He became a disciple of Hazrat Baha Uddin Zakaria of Multan. On the instruction of his Sheikh he stayed in "Uch Sharif" District Bhawalpur. Hazrat Makhdoom spent many years of his life in traveling. As such he was called Jehanian Jehan Gasht. He visited Arabia, Egypt,

Iraq, Syria, Balakh, Bukhara. During this period he performed Haj 36 times. He was, then, benefited by the company of many spiritual persons. At first he got education from his uncle Sheikh Sadar Uddin. In Multan he became a disciple of Hazrat Sheikh-ul-Islam Rukn Uddin Abdul Fatte. Then he became a disciple of Hazrat Chiragh Delhi. In the Holy Mecca he spent a lot of time in the company of Imam Abdulla Yafai and in Medina in company of Sheikh Afif Uddin Alamtari, for 2 years. He was greatly honored by Sultan Mohammed Taghlaq, who designated him Sheikh-ul-Islam and gave him Kharqa-e-Mohammadi and other gifts. He left all of them and started for Haj. Sultan Foroz Tughlaq also honored him. As such when Sultan was in Tathta in Sindh, after a defeat earlier, and was very bitter with the people over there, he at the recommendation of Hazrat Makhdoom forgave them. Sultan Feroz Tughlaq's wazir, Khan-e-Jehan was a great opponent of Hazrat Makhdoom, in the beginning, but later came around and became his disciple. This incidence is noted in Serat-ul-Arefeen. Many books have been written on Hazrat Makhdoom. Many Hindus accepted Islam under his influence, as described in the Gazetteer of Bhawalpur. The tribe of Rajputs-Kharal, besides 7 other tribes got converted to Islam, through his teachings. Among his Khalifas was his brother Raju Qattal, Sheikh Qawam Uddin of Lucknow, Sheikh Yusuf Badah, were among others besides his brother. Hazrat Makhdoom advised, in is teachings, "Recommend the victims of cruelty".

HAZRAT SHEIKH NASIR UDDIN CHIRAGH DELHI

Hazrat Sheikh Nasir Uddin Mahmud Chiragh Delhi Bin Yahyah - His father was born in Lahore but later shifted to Gudh. He was brought up by his mother. His teachers were Maulana Abdul Karim Sherwani, and Maulana Iftikhar Uddin Mohammed Gilani. At the age of 25 he started leaving worldly attachments and kept busy in prayer and worship. In early forties he came to Delhi and became a disciple of Sheikh-ul-Mashaikh Hazrat Nizam Uddin Mohammed Badauni. He used to stay with Hazrat Nizam uddin at Kelu Kheri which was at the bank of Jamuna river. He went to his home town once to serve his mother and stayed there till her death. He visited his sister too and was there occasionally, after taking permission of Hazrat Nizam Uddin. Hazrat Nizam Uddin called a few of his Khalifas on 9th November 1324 A. D., 4 months before his own death. He gave his dress, Janamaz, (Prayer Carpet) rosary, and basin to Hazrat Chiragh Delhi. These articles were gifted to him by his own "Pir", Sheikh Farid Uddin. Hazrat Chiragh Delhi lived up to 1367 A.D. nearly 32 years after the death of Hazrat Nizam Uddin and followed his teachings. His dress was stolen away by a thief, he was stabbed 11 times by his enemy, who started running. The thief was caught by his disciples, but Hazrat Chiragh Delhi stopped them from injuring the assailant. He called him closer, gave him some articles and asked him to leave. He died three years after this incident. The gifts of his "Pir" were entombed with him in his grave. - His mausoleum was built by Sultan Feroz Shah. He was not in favor of"Sama" and avoided it.

He did not write any book, but his servant Hamid Qalandari, collected his writings and gave it a form of book "Khair-ul-Majalis. Hazrat Chiragh Delhi is famous for his sayings such as: (1) One who keeps himself busy in remembering God, God is with him; (2) Keep awake at night as in those hours the light of God often shows up; (3) One who keeps himself away from sin, starts relishing this practice, (4) A godly man who keeps himself interested in prayers, they become his nourishment and food; (5) If you want worldly things for righteous and good cause, it really means a desire for the good in life after death; (6) The heart is like Kaba of God-the-Great. If Kaba of heart turns away from Qibla, then prayer is not possible.

HAZRAT KHWAJA OBED ULLAH AHRAR

Hazrat Khwaja Obed Ullah Ahrar - He was a great Sufi saint, born in 806 H in Tashqand. He died in 895 H in Samarqand and is buried there. His father's name was Khwaja Mahmud and his grandfather was Hazrat Shahab Uddin who too was a great Sufi and a disciple in spiritualism of Hazrat Qasim Tabrezi and Maulana Saad Uddin Kashgari. His grandfather predicted Khwaja Obed Ullah Ahrar's religious achievements and fame. On his mother's side Kh. Ahrar's ancestory goes up to Hazrat Umar Faruq. The famous poet Maulana Abdul Rehman

---

Incidentally Hazrat Khwaja Obed Ullah Ahrar was an ancestor of the writer of this book Ref. Tazkiratul - Khwajgan - 1944 by Hakim Khwaja Ahsan Ullah Khan. Later on the hereditary title of a Khan" was given by the Moghul Emperor Shahjehan to Hakim Kh. Fazal and Hakim Kh. Ajmal the first progeny of Kh. Obed Ullah Ahrar, practising "TIB".

Jami, who was his great friend, has written verses, in his praise, after the death of Kh. Ahrar.

The Khwaja's father was a man of meager means. He was a farmer at Gulshan. Khwaja, as such spent his early period in poverty. During Winter months he was only half dressed. His house was below the road level, so that the rain water used to collect into it. But ultimately Khwaja became a man of influence and material wealth too. However, he never forgot his early days and developed a keen concern for the poor and destitutes.

On his return from Herat, after meeting many saints, he took to the cultivation. Initially he had only a pair of bullocks, shared by a partner. By God's grace and his own hard work, he became the owner of 3,300 villages and many farms. The tax (Ushar) given by Khwaja to Sultan Ahmad Mirza was 8000 mauds of corn. On the basis of the life of Khwaja from poverty to plenty, his disciple and friend Maulana Jami recorded the above verses in Persian. Inspite of wealth and prosperity he was not attached to worldly things. He considered the secret of happiness lay in contentment. . In the history of NAQSHBANDY order no saint had so much land and wealth. Even then, he was humble and courteous to all. He did not like pride at all and considered it to be a bad habit.

Among the virtues of Khwaja was his sympathy and practical help to the sick. When an epidemic broke out in Samaqand, Khwaja looked after devoutly, the patients and did not hesitate to wash the dirty linen of the beds. So much so that he himself fell a victim to the prevalent disease. In Khwaja's eyes, a person was cruel if he did not show sympathy to men in distress and pain. Khwaja was not cruel to animals too. Khwaja thought that the spiritual goal can be achieved through service to mankind. Incidentally it may be that quality inherited by his progeny that after just a few generations "TIB" became the main profession of the progeny, till modern times, when medical doctors have come up in Khwaja's progeny.

He was highly respected by all, including princes. Babar's father Umar Sheikh Mirza was his disciple. Babar too had a regard for Khwaja's spiritual powers. He translated into Turkish language the treatise of Khwaja"'Risaliyya Waladiyya".

Kh. Obed Ullah Ahrar used to say:

(1) Do not misunderstand the holy persons (Darwesh);

(2) True Muslins are never timid or coward;

(3) There is great reward (from God) in serving those who are acquiring education;

(4) Haughtiness and pride should be disdained;

(5) Service to mankind can lead to spiritual development;

(6) A man is cruel if his heart does not throb in sympathy of those in distress and pain;

(7) Cruelty to animals is not justified;

(8) Do not attach your heart to the worldly things;

(9) There could be development of man after death (Taraqqi baad al-maut);

(10) Fossils and rocks have life and respond to human activity;

(11) Remember God at all times. Dhikre (rememberance God) should permiate one's whole body. This does not mean cutting of oneself off, from society & meditating & praying all the time in a corner;

(12) One should dress properly;

(13) Be faithful to your shaikh and rely on him;

(14) Oral communication (with common men) is more important than spiritual communication; (15) To subordinate all actions to supreme ideal and infuse spirit in all actions is the real work of a mystic.

HAZRAT MAULANA JAMI

HAZRAT MAULANA JAMI - From 817 H/1414 to 898 H/1494 A.D. His full name was Nur Uddin Abdul Rehman. He was a great Sufi, a learned man and a poet of fame. He was born in Jam, district of Khurasan. His father's name was Nizam Uddin Ahmad. He went to Hirat and Samarqand with his father. These were centers of Islamic learning. He got his spiritual education from Hazrat Bah Uddin Naqshbandi, the originator of Naqshbandi cult. He performed Haj in 877 H/1472 A.D. and returned to Hirat after a long tour of Hamadan, Kurdistan, Baghdad, Karbala, Najaf, Damascus and Tabrez. He was honored by the King, though he never mixed with him. According to Shahan_Shah Baber, nobody was comparable to Hazrat Jami in learning. In the ninth century Hijri, his reputation reached Turkey and Mohammad, the second)wanted him at Istambol.

He died in Hirat. Maulana Jami wrote many books and Mathnavi as well. It shows that he was master in different subjects. His prose was equally of high standard as his poetry.

Hazrat Jami was attached to spirituality from the age of five, when he saw Khwaja Parsa. He remembered his grandeur through his life. H. Jami elucidated the concept of"Wahdat-ulWajud"-Oneness of the Being. It was like the concept of Sheikh Kh. Obed Ullah Ahrar, who followed, Ibn Arabi & Maulana Rum in this concept. H. Jasmi's work 'Nafahat-al Uns has preserved the account of many saints of Central Asia & Persia. He believed that the Cosmic Love (Ishq Haqiqi) was necessary for the spiritual advancement.

HAZRAT SARMAD

HAZRAT SARMAD - His real name was Mohammed Saeed. He was a great Sufi, born in 1618 A.D. in a Jew family. He became a Muslim in Asfahan. Thereafter he went along with a business caravan to Tattha. There he fell in love, which changed his style of life. He distributed all his wealth to poor and came to Lahore. Then in 1056 H / 1646, he went to Hyderabad Deccan where he was greatly honored by the Ruler of Golkunda. He became his teacher. After the assassination of Dara Shikoh, his opponents declared him a heretic. Therefore he was brought to Delhi as a prisoner, where Mulla Qava, who was Justice (Qazi), gave him penalty of death. Sarmad was hanged in public in front of Jama Masjid Delhi. His grave is in the vicinity of the Masjid. This all happened in the time of Emperor Aurangzeb.

BIBLIOGRAPHY

(1) TADHKIRATUL AULIA — By Hazrat Farid Uddin Attar Urdu Translation by Dr. Banke Bihari

(2) MUSLIM SAINTS AND MYSTICS — By J.J. Arberry Commentary & Translation of Tadhkiratul-Aulia published by Penguin Group London

(3) MATHNAWI (in 6 volumes) Persian Language — By Hazrat Maulana Jalal Uddin Rumi

(4) MATHNAWI (in Persian language) — By Hazrat bu Ali Qalander

(5) KASHFUL-MAHJUB — By Hazrat Data Ganj Baksh Urdu Translation,

Medina Book Depot. Karachi

(6) FAWAID-UL-FAWAD) — From Hazrat Kh. Nizam Uddin Aulia Urdu Translation by Hazrat Kh. Hasan Nizami Sani-Delhi

(7) HIKAYAT-e-SUFIA — By Talib Hashim-Shua-e-Adab Lahore

(8) ISLAMI ENCYCLOPEDIA — By Qasim Mahmud-Shahkar Book Foundation. Karachi

(9) THE LANTERN OF THE PATH — By Hazrat Jafer-al-Sidiq - Published in English by Elementary Book Ltd. Dorsel U.K.

(10) BABA FARID — Pakistan Book Publications

(11) SINDH'S SUFI SAINT — By Sheikh Parvaiz Amin Naqshbandy

(12) TAZKIRATUL KHWAJGAN — By Hakim Kh. Ahsan Ullah Khan